Russell Library
Middletown, CT 06457

A2140 176344 1

W9-AAC-589

StreetSmart Marketing

StreetSmart Marketing

Jeff Slutsky
with Marc Slutsky

658.8
SLU

MAR 2 1990

WILEY

John Wiley & Sons, Inc.

New York • Chichester • Brisbane • Toronto • Singapore

RUSSELL LIBRARY
123 BROAD STREET
MIDDLETOWN, CT 06457

Publisher: Stephen Kippur
Editor: Katherine Schowalter
Managing Editor: Frank Grazioli
Editing, Design, and Production: Publications Development Company

This publication is designed to provide accurate and authoritative information
in regard to the subject matter covered. It is sold with the understanding
that the publisher is not engaged in rendering legal, accounting, or other
professional service. If legal advice or other expert assistance is required,
the services of a competent professional person should be sought. FROM A
DECLARATION OF PRINCIPLES JOINTLY ADOPTED BY A COMMITTEE OF
THE AMERICAN BAR ASSOCIATION AND A COMMITTEE OF PUBLISHERS.

Copyright © 1989 by Jeff Slutsky

All rights reserved. Published simultaneously in Canada.

Reproduction or translation of any part of this work beyond that permitted
by section 107 or 108 of the 1976 United States Copyright Act without the
permission of the copyright owner is unlawful. Requests for permission
or further information should be addressed to the Permission Department,
John Wiley & Sons, Inc.

Library of Congress Cataloging-in-Publication Data

Slutsky, Jeff, 1956–
 StreetSmart marketing.

 Bibliography: p.
 1. Marketing. 2. Advertising. 3. Direct marketing.
4. Advertising, Direct-mail. I. Slutsky, Marc.
II. Title. III. Title: Streetsmart marketing.
HF5415.122.S58 1989 658.8 88-28037
ISBN 0-471-61883-7
ISBN 0-471-61882-9 (pbk.)

Printed in the United States of America

89 90 10 9 8 7 6 5 4 3 2

This book is dedicated to and in loving memory
of our father, Alan Slutsky—from whom we received
our warped sense of humor.

TRADEMARKS

Fruit-of-the-Loom is the trademark of Fruit-of-the-Loom.
Playtex is the trademark of Playtex.
GE is the trademark of General Electric.
Serta Perfect Sleeper is the trademark of Serta.
Nautilus is the trademark of Nautilus.
minit-lube is the trademark of Quaker State.
Dairy Queen is the trademark of Dairy Queen.
Skippers is the trademark of Skippers.
AT&T Phone Centers is the trademark of American Telephone and Telegraph.
Chick-fil-A is the trademark of Chick-fil-A, Inc.
Arby's is the trademark of Arby's, Inc.
Baskin Robbins is the trademark of Baskin Robbins.
RainierBank is the trademark of Rainier Bank, Inc.
Western Auto is the trademark of Western Auto.
McDonald's is the trademark of McDonald's Corporation.
Carpetland, USA is the trademark of Carpetland, USA, Inc.
Pizza Hut is the trademark of Pizza Hut, Inc.
FTD is the trademark of FTD, Inc.
CBS is the trademark of Columbia Broadcasting Company.
ABC is the trademark of American Broadcasting Company.
Pepsi is the trademark of Pepsi Cola Bottling Company.
Taco Bell is the trademark of Taco Bell International.
Great Clips is the trademark of Great Clips, Inc.
IBM is the trademark of International Business Machines.
TeleMagic is the trademark of Remote Control, Inc.
Pizza King is the trademark of Pizza King, Inc.
Famous Recipe Fried Chicken is the trademark of Shoney's, Inc.
Shell is the trademark of Shell Oil Company.
Subway is the trademark of Subway Sandwich & Subs.
Wags Family Restaurants is the trademark of Marriott Corporation.

Preface

A marketing executive once remarked, "I know I'm wasting half of my advertising budget, but I don't know which half." Most business people agree with this, but while 50 percent may have been true a few years ago, today the percentage of wasted advertising dollars is in the 75–90 percent range.

Advertising and promotion cost more and deliver less. Television rates soar in the face of declining and fragmented viewership. Newspaper rates skyrocket as readership falls. According to *The Wall Street Journal*, corporations, big and small, are in a panic because their advertising and marketing are just not working for them. Advertising agencies are in a frenzy trying to figure out alternative ways to give their clients a better return on their advertising dollars.

Consumers are not responding to mass advertising as they once did. Perhaps this is because their tastes have become more regionalized, individualized, and personalized. Corporations are only just learning how to appeal to the individual tastes of consumers, but they are still at a loss when it comes to marketing to them.

The authors of best selling books, including *In Search of Excellence, Passion for Excellence,* and *Reinventing the Corporation,* have stressed and pleaded for corporations to get in touch with the needs of their customers. Only then can they survive. Street-Smart Marketing shows you how.

You can't necessarily increase your profits by increasing your advertising budget. Some companies are using new approaches to supplement traditional advertising. Direct response mailings, telemarketing, publicity campaigns, and sweepstakes are being tried. This is, perhaps, a step in the right direction, but they are still missing a tremendous opportunity. Now is the time to out-think your competition instead of out-spending them.

It took over 10 years to develop this simple approach. Any corporation or small business can adapt it to create marketing and advertising that generates results. One simple underlying principle makes all the difference in the world. This principle is explained in the following example of a marketing program for a fast food unit that was in trouble.

A top level fast-food restaurant was having trouble with one of its stores in a little town in Ohio, about 45 miles from Columbus. In this small town, this restaurant had always done a brisk business until the summer of 1987. That spring, a second store in the chain opened on the other side of town near the interstate. Management expected some sales loss to their old store, but they didn't count on competing chains also opening up in the same small town.

Despite running a tight ship and turning out a super product, sales dropped. The pie could only be divided into so many pieces. We were contacted as consultants and given three months to work on the problem. We trained one employee, who was both a crew member and a breakfast hostess, to set up several customer-generating promotions in the community.

Using her streetsmart marketing techniques, she arranged with 14 of the 15 major employers in the city to give each one of their employees a special Employee VIP Card to the chain. The local Chamber of Commerce mailed out, at their own expense, 12,000 VIP cards to its members and their employees. Dozens of area merchants distributed advertising to their customers for free. Even the local elementary school distributed special invitations for the students to visit the restaurant with their parents.

In just 90 days, according to their Regional Advertising Supervisor, sales increased by 21 percent. This was better than they had ever dreamed possible under the competitive circumstances.

This example demonstrates two very important lessons:

1. You get more results from your advertising and marketing efforts if you carry those efforts all the way to the final point of distribution, whether it be a store, dealer, agent, or office.

2. In order to be truly effective, the execution of these programs must take place on the neighborhood level by the person or persons who run the operation in that neighborhood. If execution comes from any form of supervisory level, the impact and ability to dominate the neighborhood is lost.

Even a Fortune 500 company made up of over thousands of individual locations and serving thousands of individual neighborhoods is run by thousands of *individual* store managers who have the potential of making a tremendous difference in the sales volume of their stores if they are properly trained and motivated.

Another classic example follows:

In 1979, we were working with six different pizza franchisees who, between them, owned and operated 300 stores. This company seemed to have very little interest, at that time, in localized marketing in any shape or form; but once the word got out about sales increases and turnarounds in stores that had been losing money, the rest of their franchise store owners (about 2000 stores) wanted our streetfighting program.

Feeling the pressure from their franchisees, this client developed their own local store marketing program and launched it during their annual marketing convention. Their program consisted primarily of a single manual in a fancy binder. It put more emphasis on the "glitz" than the "guts"; it even came in its own carrying case. In their effort to create the cute packaging, they forgot to create programs that store owners and managers could use. This is the main principle of streetsmart marketing:

Customers tend to ignore expensive mass marketing
by mass marketeers that fail to appeal to their
customer's specific localized needs.

or conversely stated:

Neighborhood customers respond to neighborhood
marketing conducted by neighborhood
business people.

Corporations are looking for an edge over their competitors. You can get this edge by focusing on the community level. You need to adapt your marketing to your neighborhoods. The chapters that follow are a "how-to" lesson, regardless of your size, to think small in order to reach your customers where they live—in their neighborhoods. An added benefit of this streetsmart approach is that it can be done on a limited budget.

Acknowledgments

The authors acknowledge the contributions of various friends and associates who enriched the pages of this book with their guidance, wisdom, advice, and support—among them: Bill Bishop; Eugene Hameroff; Jeff Herman, a great literary agent; Ron Kaatz; Michael LeBoeuf; Dorothy Leeds; Mark Sanborn; Robert Shook; Steve Simon; George Walther; Stacy; every member of the National Speakers Association; and our family: Rick (Rendsel), Howard (Head), Charlotte (Mommy), and Jodi (Dinkette).

Contents

Confessions of a Streetfighter: A Lesson in Chutzpah

Imagine for a moment that you own an appliance store. Customers come to your store and look at a refrigerator, freezer, or perhaps a range. They spend an hour or so getting information and haggling over the price, then tell you that they "want to think about it." Of course, you know that means that they want to go across the street to a mall where there are major retailers who also sell appliances; then they price shop for awhile. They waste some more time down the street at the regional competitors, and finally, after a few quick visits to some local competition, they have finished their competitive shopping marathon. By then they have totally forgotten that you exist.

This actually happened to a streetfighter client of mine in Fort Wayne, Indiana. He said that customers were price shopping him to death, and he wanted to know if there was anything that could be done about it. How could he make sure that he was the last place they shopped, or at least narrow their choices to two or three so he had a fighting chance of getting the sale?

We had him do several things. One was to plug in one of his freezers and fill it with half gallons of ice cream.

A customer would come in and look at a refrigerator, freezer, or a new range. If they said, "We want to think about it" (which in the language of "customereese" translates into, "We're not buying from you"), the sales staff was instructed to give that customer a half gallon of ice cream just for stopping in.

Naturally, their hearts melt with enthusiasm for the store—but that's not all. The customer is ready to get in the car on a hot and humid day. Heat fumes rise from the hood. The car door is opened and heat escapes from inside the car as if opening that new electric oven they just priced. The windows are rolled down and they gingerly slide onto the hot seat, while placing the cold half gallon of premium vanilla ice cream further in the middle.

Condensation forms on the cold container. The engine comes to life and the car air conditioner spews forth hot air at first, followed by warm, then finally cooling, relief. Their minds clear. At that point, they realize they have a dilemma on their hands—the result of which is to take their ice cream home immediately, thus keeping them from further shopping the competition. Later that week, the store delivers their new electric range.

This is called streetfighting, and its concepts form the basis for *StreetSmart Marketing*.

The streetsmart approach to local marketing is a combination of results-oriented, low cost, and local store promotional techniques that are integrated with entrepreneurial spirit, cleverness, and nerve. In this first chapter, you'll discover some interesting examples of the streetfighter's attitude. These are unusual promotions that illustrate a unique form of business street-savvy and creative problem solving.

The stories in this chapter are not necessarily meant for you to apply directly, but rather are meant to start you thinking. They're the catalyst in the mixture that creates the concrete foundation of this program. Armed with new knowledge, you will have the potential to dramatically increase your sales. You will begin to understand the novel psyche and psychology of the streetfighter that allows you to out-think your competition, not out-spend them.

It is the goal of this chapter to set the stage for discovering, developing, and distributing your own customized, results-oriented, local marketing program. It's up to you to determine for yourself just how competitive and aggressive you want to be.

Some of these examples fall into a grey area that may cross over a line that makes you feel uncomfortable. This is understandable. There are a few examples that I would never recommend, yet the lesson learned from them offers valuable insight. Take them in the spirit for which they're intended—open your eyes to different and new possibilities.

TAKING A TOLL

This example is from a book called *The Great Brain Robbery*, self-published by Murray Raphel and Ray Considine. (See Bibliography.) A stockbroker on the East Coast, commuting to work daily, paid a toll twice each working day. Before he paid his toll, he would look in his rearview mirror. If he saw a Lincoln, Cadillac, Mercedes, or Rolls Royce, he would pay not only his toll, but also that of the person behind him. He then left his business card with the tollbooth attendant.

The guy in the Mercedes would pull up with a dollar bill in his hand, only to be informed that the person in the car ahead of him had already paid his toll. The attendant would then give the puzzled driver the business card left behind by the stockbroker.

He got more new clients from a dollar toll than from anything else he did.

I know what you're thinking. What does that have to do with me? Perhaps you are not a stockbroker, or you do not pay a toll to get to work.

StreetSmart Marketing Principle 1

Always be on the lookout for opportunities,
and be ready to seize them.

Keep an "eyes-open, ears-to-the-ground" attitude. You never know where an opportunity to increase your sales will spring up. It could even be in the rearview mirror; it will often occur in the most unlikely places. As a streetfighter, you must always be prepared to take advantage of every window of opportunity before that window closes on you.

StreetSmart Marketing Principle 2

Don't try to reinvent the wheel; instead,
make small improvements on existing successful programs.

A streetfighter truly believes that there is nothing new under the sun. It has all been done before. The success comes in recognizing these effective ideas regardless of the source. It may be in your industry or in a completely unrelated industry. Once you identify the idea, then you must extract the element of that idea which has merit for you. Next you modify, improve, and adapt the idea to make it work for you.

In a sense, this entire book is an illustration of the second streetsmart principle. You will not read new ideas, but new adaptations of old ideas. These are combined with other ideas and presented in an easily understood manner. Some of these ideas are modifications and improvements from my first book, *Streetfighting: Low Cost Advertising/Promotion for Your Small Business*, while other ideas came from other sources. It doesn't have to be new or unique to be good—it only has to work.

StreetSmart Marketing Principle 3

When you see something that works for
someone else—borrow it!

Why spend thousands of dollars and hours on formulating new ideas? After all, there are none. Just find someone who has an idea that you need, then use it.

That's exactly what a lawn and garden operator did in Texas. He heard the tollbooth story, but he knew that the idea really didn't apply to him. He wasn't a stockbroker, nor did he live on the East Coast. He didn't have to pay a toll to get to work. Yet, there was something about the story that inspired him.

No, they didn't have tollbooths, but they did have something in their downtown area that was very annoying to many of his customers and potential customers: parking meters. This gave him an idea.

He created a promotional piece that looked remarkably like the local parking ticket. It was the same size and color. It read, "This is not a parking ticket. However, we happened to be going by your car and noticed that your meter was ready to run out or had already done so. To help you avoid the hassle and expense of paying a $5 fine, we've taken the liberty of putting a little money in the meter for you. Compliments of [and you could just as easily insert your company name here]."

As you can imagine, it created quite a lot of attention. Many people talked about it. The lawn and garden operator received a lot of phone calls—including one from the local police department. Apparently, they have a policy not to ticket the same car twice. The officers were heading downtown ready to get their quota for the day, but all of the cars looked ticketed.

It was costing the city a lot of money.

One day he received an irate call from the police department. The officer he spoke to was not pleased. He explained to the officer that he checked with his attorney before making the tickets, and it was a perfectly legal promotion. "It may be perfectly legal, sir, but need I remind you that you do have seven registered vehicles on my streets, and I'm sure if my boys look real close, they might be able to find some . . ."

"Say no more." Then he started asking the officer some questions. He knew that when you have an irate customer, you don't battle; you ask questions. In doing so, you not only find out what the problem is, but by probing and digging with your questions, they'll usually offer you their own solution. Not only that, but it helps you remain in control of the conversation as opposed to constantly trying to defend yourself. We'll discuss this in greater detail in later chapters.

By asking questions, our streetfighter found out about the confusion and the cost to the city in lost revenue. Wanting to remain in control of the conversation while helping the officer to suggest his own solution, he continued, "Let me ask you this. If I changed the color of my promotional piece from red to yellow, would your officers be able to tell the difference between the two?"

"Is that a trick question? Of course they would."

"And if they could tell the difference between the two, our problem is solved. Right?"

"I suppose it would be."

"Fair enough," he responded, and with that he was able to turn a potential disaster into a successful promotion responsible for getting him many new clients without spending a great deal of money or alienating the law enforcement officers.

StreetSmart Marketing Principle 4

Never give up, even when confronted with an apparent major disaster or hopeless situation. A streetfighter adapts and overcomes until success is achieved.

The reason you have to have a streetsmart approach to your marketing is because advertising just doesn't work like it once did. One of the biggest problems is that there is so much advertising (or clutter, as advertising people are fond of referring to it) that most people just tune it out. We are exposed to hundreds of advertising messages every day. One article suggests that we are exposed to over 1700 commercial messages each day. From the minute you wake up in the morning and put on your Fruit-Of-The-Looms or cross your heart with Playtex until you go to bed at night and pop out your Bausch & Lomb contact lenses, set your GE alarm clock and jump in your Serta Perfect Sleeper, you are constantly bombarded with advertising.

You can't remember all of this advertising, so your brain protects you by tuning out all but a very small number of these messages. One of the goals of *StreetSmart Marketing* is to create advertising that is not perceived as advertising and therefore provides a greater opportunity for the message to have retention, recall, and response.

A HAZARD WITH THE DUKE

This next idea was used by a restaurant in Kentucky, and I highly recommend that you do *not* use it. It illustrates a precaution: Once you start to get into the swing of things, you may have a tendency to go overboard. You must be aware of those grey areas as mentioned earlier and not cross over into an area that can backfire on you. At the same time, you can't be afraid to take a chance. You can learn more from your failures than from your successes.

A number of years ago, the manager of a "fern bar" type restaurant noticed that Tuesday was a very bad day for him, and he tried all kinds of promotions for building it up, but to no avail. One day he was thumbing through the local phone book and happened to come across a local person whose name was John Wayne.

He telephoned the local Mr. Wayne and informed him that his name was selected at random out of the local telephone book, and that he had just won a dinner for two at his restaurant the next Tuesday evening at 8:00 P.M. John Wayne was delighted, and he agreed to be there with his wife to get their free dinner.

✓ The next day a huge sign was placed in front of the restaurant announcing, "John Wayne to Dine Here Next Tuesday."

It created quite a stir, and when Tuesday came, it was the busiest evening in the restaurant's history. By 6:00 P.M. there was actually a waiting line to get seated for dinner. By 7:00 P.M. the waiting line was out the front door, and by 8:00 P.M. that waiting line was almost to the street.

Then came the announcement over the loudspeaker: "Ladies and Gentlemen—Mr. John Wayne."

Silence filled the room. There stood John, a good old Kentucky farmboy complete with bib overalls, a Massey Fergeson baseball cap, and his wife at his side.

The manager began to think that he may have gone a little bit too far with this one. He looked at all the possible methods of escape from the room. Then everyone in the place, realizing what had happened, burst out laughing. They ushered John and his wife to their seats. They asked him for his autograph, and they had their pictures taken with him.

It was a tremendously successful promotion, but it could just as easily have scarred the business for life. I personally like the idea so much that I briefly thought of using it in the town I live in now. Instead of John Wayne, I was able to come up with a George Burns, a Tim Conway, two Richard Simmons, a couple of Robert Conrads, 3 William Conrads, 3 Michael Jacksons, 19 Don Johnsons, and 257 Mr. Rogers!

◇

THE BOURBON COWBOY

I used a similar idea for a nightclub I partly owned one time. It was about the time when the movie *Urban Cowboy* came out, and the newest fad in bars was the mechanical bull. Our club was a disco-type place, but in a small town you compete with all the bars. Word had gone out that one of the other places had one of these $8000 monstrosities on order, and we knew the novelty of a mechanical bull could be a serious threat.

We went into action.

We sent out a press release, well in advance of the competitor's bull debut, announcing the debut of the area's first mechanical *horse!* This mechanical horse was not to be confused with a mechanical bull, since the horse was specifically designed for the purposes of amusement, while the bull was actually a training device for professional rodeo participants. To the best of our knowledge, there was never an injury in a single nightclub with our particular model.

The night of the promotion, our club was packed wall-to-wall with customers, news-team minicams, and photographers. The event was cosponsored by the local country music radio station, which dubbed the program "Bourbon Cowboy Night" because all bourbon drinks were on special. The unveiling was planned for 10:00 P.M., and the anticipation was tremendous.

The disk jockey from the sponsoring local country radio station put on the old hit song, "Back in the Saddle Again." As it played, he ducked behind the curtain and jumped on the horse as the curtain was lifted. And there it was—our mechanical horse. Just like the kind you would find in front of a supermarket that a kid could ride for a quarter.

Everyone laughed and had a great time with our little joke except one cowboy who drove about 300 miles to practice for a rodeo. He was angry. It took close to a case of bourbon to calm him down. The next day, he peaceably got back in his pickup and drove off into the sunrise.

It was certainly somewhat risky, but we were able to pull it off. It allowed us to kick off our "Every Tuesday Bourbon Cowboy Promotion" with the station that turned a dead night into a night of reasonable sales. Furthermore, it took some of the steam out of the competition when they did debut their "bull" some weeks later. Their promotion just never got all of the excitement that it might have if we hadn't done our "promotional vaccination" first. Even when the local newspaper did a full-page spread featuring their "bull," a portion of the article featured our "horsey" as a safer alternative!

Even though both of these last two promotions got their desired results, they did so under very special circumstances. You must be careful to know just how far you can go, which rules to bend, and how far to bend them. There is a point where it's no longer worth it. You have to determine for yourself what that point is for you and your organization. That brings us to the next streetfighting rule:

StreetSmart Marketing Principle 5

Don't gamble, but do take calculated risks.

In business, you take risks all the time while trying to minimize your potential losses and maximize your potential gains. You must take risks to develop a local store marketing program that really works, and you will have some failures. It's part of the game, but you'll have plenty of success stories, too, and your program will grow.

UPPING YOURS THREE WAYS

There are three basic ways to increase sales: (1) get more customers; (2) get your customers to visit you more often; and (3) get your customers to spend more during each visit. Your streetsmart marketing program discusses all three. The following case is an example of the third concept.

GETTING CREAMED FOR A BIGGER PIECE OF THE PIE

This is another restaurant example. This particular restaurant served, without a doubt, the best banana cream pies in the world. Yet, they sold very little banana cream pie. Their dessert sales in general were low. So the manager ran a contest. The server who sold the most banana cream pies during the month would win an entire banana cream pie—and get to throw it in the manager's face! You've never seen such a motivated crew in your life.

These servers really wanted to push those pies. They would ask the customers if they wanted pie for dessert. They suggested pie for dessert. They would bring a piece over for the customer to see just how wonderful it was. They were even selling whole pies to go!

The result of the contest was that it increased dessert sales for the month by 50 percent. Keep in mind that these are added sales and added profit, not trading one item for another. Interestingly enough, the long-term results after the contest ended was a 20 percent increase in dessert sales. The servers experienced for themselves just how easy it was to sell dessert, and they had a lot of fun in the process. Their customers perceived this as quality service, and their tips reflected it.

StreetSmart Marketing Principle 6

Don't out-spend your competition; out-think them.

While this particular principle is a common theme for the entire streetsmart marketing concept, there are some specific examples of battling your competition. You must look for every opportunity to do everything better than them; you will also often have opportunities to do battle directly with them.

A LITTLE HOT AIR PUTS THE COMPETITION ON ICE

A video appliance store in Colorado was reasonably successful for a number of years. It was a small family business featuring VCRs and big screen TVs, as well as the more traditional audio/video lines. They made a nice living and never really had to hustle much until a major regional competitor moved to town.

This competitor was building a major store just a few blocks from theirs, and it seemed as if they had an unlimited advertising budget. When it came time for this major competitor to have their grand opening extravaganza, they spared no expense. Full-page newspapers ads, radio, and TV all promoted the grand opening of this new store.

The smaller store felt beaten. How could this Mom-and-Pop operation compete with such a major company with a seemingly unlimited advertising budget? This was a true-to-life "David and Goliath" story. What this merchant needed to compete was a promotional sling. This came in the form of a miniature helium blimp that the small store flew above their own store the day of the Grand Opening of their competition. They put some streamers and other decorations out in their small parking lot, and on their reader board near the road you could read: Now Open.

They didn't say "Grand Opening" but "Now Open," which was true! Half the people got confused and went to the smaller store by accident. It was the most successful promotion they ever ran—all at the expense of their new competitor.

RIPPING OUT THE COMPETITION

When a large pizza chain came to Denver, they made it very difficult for all of the other pizza delivery stores in the area. This particular pizza chain, once established in a market, was a tough act to beat. One of the more important advertising media for the pizza delivery business is the Yellow Pages. After all, when you're looking for a place that delivers pizza, that is the logical place to look.

One of the local pizza delivery chains waited until the new Yellow Pages came out, then ran a promotion: "Bring us our competitor's Yellow Page ad out of the phone book, and we'll give you two-for-one pizza!"

Everyone was ripping out the Yellow Page ad of the competition and bringing them in. That's real streetfighting.

IN THE PINK

There have been some interesting ways in which businesses have dealt with competition over the years. One that comes to mind is the story about the rivalry between the canners and distributors of pink salmon and those of red salmon. Unlike all of the other examples mentioned so far where I was either personally involved or knew the person who was, I was never able to trace the origin of this story to see how true it was; yet, whether it's fact or fable (or a little of both), I think it illustrates the streetfighter's attitude of "out-thinking" your competition.

According to the story, pink salmon outsold red salmon by a huge margin. The red salmon folks were not too happy about this, so they called their marketing team to the executive offices for a major pow-wow. "You have 90 days to start closing the gap on pink salmon, or you'll be given your pink slips!"

They were motivated. Three months passed, and sales began to climb. It was a definite move forward, so the executives let them continue for another few months. By the end of the fifth month, they realized it was no fluke, but a real upward trend in sales. They brought their marketing team up to the executive suite for a little cocktail party, to be followed by a marketing presentation. They wanted to know the reason for their new-found success.

After the champagne, caviar, and red salmon croquettes, the head of the marketing team was asked to explain exactly how they were able to reverse their sales trends.

He simply answered, "We redesigned the label on our cans."

"That's it? You have to be kidding. You change our label and sales go up?" There was quite a commotion among the executives until a couple of the marketing assistants placed a large mock-up of the new label design on an easel for them all to see. The label read, "Authentic Norwegian Red Salmon, *Guaranteed Not to Turn Pink.*"

SLIGHT OF VAN

An electrician in the Chicago area was razzed by some of his poker buddies one night because he had only one truck for his small company, which was comprised primarily of him, his son, and his wife.

"Well, if they're impressed by having a fleet of trucks," he thought to himself, "I'll give them a fleet of trucks." So on the right side of his truck he had painted, "Unit #3." On the left side it read, "Unit #4." On the back it read, "Unit #5."

His buddies never gave him a hard time again.

As you start to get involved with much of the "nuts and

bolts" of local marketing in later chapters, you'll find that this streetsmart principle becomes one of the most important:

StreetSmart Marketing Principle 7

Create an "everyone-wins" situation.

The only possible exception to this rule is, of course, your competition.

FULL HOUSE

The first time I told this next story to a reporter, I got in trouble. The reporter insisted that I was deceiving the public, but no matter how I tried to explain that it was an effective yet harmless promotion, the reporter kept blasting me about it. I haven't used it much since, even though I think it's a good story. As far as marketing techniques go, I doubt if there's much direct application to most operations, yet it's the cleverness of this solution that impressed me. An account executive who worked at the public relations company who handled my publicity told me about a restaurant in a large metropolitan area that placed a small ad in the entertainment section of the newspaper. Even though it was a reasonably small ad, it was still expensive, because in a large city, the circulation is high.

The small ad announced the opening of an elegant new restaurant where you could expect the finest delicacies that were prepared to perfection by a team of world-renowned chefs. Reservations were a must. No address was given; only the phone number to reserve your table.

The small ad got responses; many people called, but they were immediately informed that the restaurant was so busy that they could not possibly take their reservations. As a matter of fact, the maitre'd said he could not take a reservation for at least three weeks and to please call back at that time. The ad continued to run about once a month, and people called and were asked to call back two or three weeks later because they were so busy.

After a couple of months of this, many people were talking about this restaurant. It was creating quite a stir, yet everyone had difficulty getting reservations. "It must be a wonderful place; I can't remember when it took so long to get into a restaurant."

After about three months and numerous attempts by hundreds of people, they were finally given their reservations . . . and their expectations were met. The establishment was everything they dreamed of and more—including being popular. Those without reservations waited hours, and this was early in the week when most places are lucky to fill a third of their tables. This restaurant was obviously a big success.

What they didn't know was that it had been under construction for those first three months.

As a result of their clever use of a small newspaper ad, the restaurant owners were able to create tremendous interest and word-of-mouth advertising long before they opened. To make that kind of impact with a more traditional approach would have cost them 10 to 20 percent more in traditional advertising.

At no time did they lie. When they got calls, they said they were "busy." They were—they were busy painting and hammering.

Did everyone win? It may be a bit of a stretch, but when you really think about it, everyone did. The restaurant won because they were able to pack the place from the first day using a shoestring ad budget. But what about the consumer? To make this same impact, the owner would have spent a great deal of money in advertising. That additional expense has to be recouped somehow, whether in the price of the meals, the quality of the ingredients, the size of the portions, or the quality of the atmosphere. The less the advertising costs, the more value the owner could actually give the customer for his money. He did provide a tremendous value, so in this situation, everyone won.

DON'T BE CHICKEN—SERVE IT

When do you step over the line? That's hard to say, but I think my brother Marc (who co-authored this book) came real close when he chaired a meeting for a civic group that he had volunteered for. To insure a good attendance at his meeting, he sent out fliers to everyone in the organization and offered them a free chicken dinner if they attended this important meeting.

It worked. He had the best attendance in the history of the organization for that type of program, and when they got there, they received their free chicken dinner—little packets of dried corn!

Some people were amused, but others were upset because they had been looking forward to a real chicken dinner. Thinking fast, Marc told them that it was just a little joke and that the real food was on its way. "In the meantime," he said, "Let's get our meeting out of the way." Then he sent his co-chairperson over to a local take-out chicken place for a dozen buckets and fix'ns. Sure it cost him a few hundreds bucks—but he felt his life was worth it.

LOCKED IN ATTENDANCE

A client of ours had a similar situation. He had reasonably good attendance, but everyone kept showing up at different times. This made it very difficult to conduct the meeting. So he got a bunch of old keys from a locksmith and mailed one key to each of his committee members with a note that said, "Dear Joe, I'm going to be running a little late. Please open up for me." Everyone was there on time. None of the keys worked, but his problem was solved.

GETTING JIMMIED

Our landlord showed his streetfighting powers once when he had a problem in the neighborhood where our office building is located. It's in an area called German Village. This is just south of downtown, where the buildings were built at the turn of the century and were recently renovated. According to our landlord, when they first renovated the building we now call our corporate headquarters, some kids in the neighborhood threw rocks through all of the brand new windows.

Our landlord was reluctant to immediately replace those windows; he wanted to wait until he found a way to protect them from the vandals. He finally put a hand-painted sign on the building which stayed up through the rest of the renovation. It read, "If you break these windows, you will go to jail. Ask Jimmie Plunket!"

I asked him who Jimmie Plunket was and he said, "I don't know, but you sure don't see him around here anymore, do you?"

You can use the streetfighter's attitude to solve just about any kind of problem or to make the best of any type of situation.

LEARNING FROM A DUMMY

I once had a problem with kids, too. Before moving to Columbus, I lived in Fort Wayne in a nice house with a swimming pool. During the summer, when I would leave in the morning to go to work, the kids would sneak over my fence and go swimming in my pool. They were totally unsupervised. One neighbor told me that these kids were even jumping off of the roof of the screened-in patio into the pool. This made me very uneasy.

I talked to their parents, but that didn't help. I then talked to the police, and they couldn't help. So I decided to take matters into my own hands and use some streetfighting. I came up with an idea while watching the *Wizard of Oz*. When the scarecrow came on the screen wishing he had a brain, I thought to myself, "That's what I need—a scare-kid!"

A good friend of mine owned a children's clothing store, and I asked to borrow one of his kiddie mannequins. He agreed without hesitation, but he did look a little perplexed when I asked, "Can this thing float?"

"I suppose if you took it off its metal base, we could get it to float for you."

I took it home fully clothed and waited for a very hot day. I knew that the minute I was out of the driveway, the kids would be over the fence and into the pool. They did just that, and as they were in mid-dive, they saw this fully-clothed body floating face down in the pool.

They never came back. They never came back for Halloween. They never came back to cut my grass. One of them must have been my paperboy, because it was two months before I could get a paper delivered to the house. However, my problem was solved.

A little extreme? Perhaps. Effective? Without a doubt. Original? Absolutely not, but it was inspired.

I learned very quickly in business that the *merchandising,* as much as the *quality* of the goods and services was important to success. I had a merchandising problem in my own business. When I first started the streetfighting program I was only 24 years old. Clients wouldn't pay attention to me because of my age, even though I knew how to help them. In one case, after working for a client for three months and getting good results, my age came up in a conversation. When the client realized how young I was, he panicked and fired me.

Using my own streetfighting concepts I began to "re-package" myself. I re-evaluated how I dressed—got rid of the polyester leisure suit and wore a dark grey Armani instead. Traded my sports car for a more conservative sedan and even had the hair around my temples dyed grey.

Even with the new packaging, I was often asked my age so I had to come up with a response that would not cause me to lose my credibility and, at the same time, tell the truth. I finally came up with a streetfighter's response to the question, "By the way, Jeff, just how old are you?"

I looked them right straight in the eye and responded, "I'll be 34 in April."

True statement. (It happens to be in 1994, but it is a true statement.)

StreetSmart Marketing Principle 8

Make the most of what you have.

Sometimes you just have to deal with things that happen to you. But as a streetfighter, you don't let these little problems get in your way. Instead, you turn them into opportunities. Such was the case with my last name. Growing up with the last name of Slutsky has not been a picnic.

You can probably imagine what my nickname was. I'll give you a hint—it wasn't Ski. The first time I noticed that my last name was going to cause me a great deal of notoriety was during my sophomore year in high school. My best friend would delight in yelling down the hall of the school for me, "Hey Slut!" Very embarrassing.

It came as a great relief to find out not too long ago that my ancestors came from a small town in Russia called Sleuts. I was relieved because I also found out that last names could be based on the small town from which you came, and not necessarily on what your parents did for a living.

In looking back at all the crazy things that have happened, it's interesting to consider that the streetfighter in us helps us make the most of any situation. The rest of this book is designed to help you get the most from your marketing, advertising, and promotions by adding a new dimension to your existing marketing strategy—local store, neighborhood-level marketing.

By now, you understand a little of the attitude, and of course you'll develop more of that as you learn the step-by-step techniques and skills to becoming a streetfighter.

As you begin to develop your own program, please keep in mind that to get the most out of it, you must have fun with it. This is a very serious program, yet if you do everything you can to make it fun and exciting for those who will be trained to use it on the local level, your results will increase dramatically.

12 Ways to Isolate, Infiltrate, and Dominate Your Marketplace

2

You must know your turf—the area around your store from which you get 90 percent of your business. Depending on your type of operation and your marketplace, it could be anywhere from a three-block to a three-mile radius. If it's not geographical, then it might be demographical and comprised of a circle of specialized customers. It is up to you to identify and dominate your turf.

What's the name of the high school down the street from you? The church two blocks away? The third largest employer in your area? The most aggressive nonprofit organization? Can you name 25 retail merchants in your neighborhood and the manager of the highest volume area convenience store, dry cleaner, video store, bowling alley, and health club?

Each one of these groups can send you hundreds, if not thousands, of customers—if you approach them properly. In your neighborhood, there are hundreds of operations that are just waiting to send you new customers. You would be amazed at the wealth of opportunity you can find on your turf, and they are all free for the asking, once you know how to ask!

NEIGHBORHOOD NETWORKING

The basic idea behind streetsmart marketing is to network with every imaginable group in your community to create low-cost promotional programs that are beneficial to them while providing you a new stream of buying customers.

There are hundreds of promotional ideas and concepts that you can use in and around the community. These can be broken down into 12 different groups based on which ones will provide you with free and low-cost distribution into the community of your advertising. By the time you're done with this book, you'll know numerous ways to get free advertising.

The 12 Points of Free Distribution

1. Neighborhood businesses to their customers or clients

2. Employers to their employees

3. Associations and organizations to their members

4. Educational institutions to their students

5. Businesses-serving businesses to their customers

6. Special-event promoters to their attendees

7. Nonprofit groups to their community supporters

8. Your employees to their friends and acquaintances

9. Your customers to their friends and acquaintances

10. You to your customers

11. The news media to their readers, listeners, and viewers

12. The advertising media to their readers, listeners, and viewers

Though very similar in many ways, each of these 12 different distribution groups needs to be approached in its own special way. The specific techniques used to take advantage of these opportunities and gain the cooperation of these 12 groups is the main focus of the rest of this book.

This chapter focuses on the first half of this list. Much attention is given to the first one because once you fully understand the first, the rest are much easier.

NONADVERTISING ADVERTISING

In addition to getting your advertising distributed free and/or at low cost, one other important concept of streetsmart marketing is that you are creating advertising that is not perceived as advertising by the consumer. As mentioned earlier, consumers are inundated with advertising messages and tune out the vast majority of them as a result. Your TV commercial comes on and your potential customers head for the kitchen or the bathroom. Your radio ad comes on and the customers switch channels. Your newspaper ad ends up at the bottom of a bird cage or wrapped around the garbage.

With a streetsmart approach, however, you can create a unique environment in which your advertising message is taken seriously by your potential customers.

REINFORCEMENT, NOT REPLACEMENT; SUPPLEMENT, NOT SAVIOR

This is not to say that you shouldn't use traditional advertising. Nothing could be further from the truth. Yet, because of the decreased effectiveness of traditional advertising, streetsmart marketing is vital to supplement your marketing efforts. The more effective your traditional advertising is, the easier it is to get results from your streetsmart marketing efforts. They go hand-in-hand. You'll learn some ways to get more from traditional advertising (on a local level) in Chapter 8.

The ideas you will find in this chapter have gotten me into all kinds of trouble, especially with radio stations. The streetsmart approach teaches you how to negotiate with the radio station so you can get the most out of your local media budget.

THE NEW AND IMPROVED STREETFIGHTER PROGRAM

My last book, *Streetfighting: Low-Cost Advertising/Promotions for Your Small Business*, served as the starting point for this book. However, since *Streetfighting* was published, there have been tremendous improvements, new ideas, and approaches that warranted a completely new book.

You'll find that *StreetSmart Marketing* offers training techniques and includes proven ideas that make implementation easier and less time-consuming. Furthermore, my first book was geared primarily to smaller, independent businesses. Since that time, we've worked with many larger organizations who need to know not only how to develop the program, but also how to make it work within their corporate structure. You'll learn that in this book, as well.

GREATER EXPECTATIONS

Your *StreetSmart Marketing* program is not an overnight proposition. The techniques used are deceptively simple, but the overall game plan needed to develop and implement your program throughout your organization will take time, if you want to do it right. It may take anywhere from six months to two or more years to get it fully operational. This will depend on the size and structure of your organization.

The reason the program is worth the time and effort is because once your program is running and properly administered, it will produce results forever. It's a commitment that potentially offers you a very high payback.

YOU HAVE TO KISS A LOT OF FROGS

You'll find that developing this program specifically for your operation will involve trial and error. Not every cross promotion or community involvement program you do is going to give you an immediate profit. The majority of the programs will bring in some results, but it's the accumulated results over a period of time that make these programs worthwhile. In baseball, you hit some singles and a few doubles. You get a triple once in awhile, and perhaps even a home run. You also strike out; but in the end, someone wins the game.

It's the sum total of all the *StreetSmart Marketing* tactics, used over a period of time, that gets results and increases profits. If you're looking for quick and easy results, this program is not for you. But if you give it the time and effort it needs, you'll get the results you want.

PUMPING UP THE PROFITS

Here's an example of one of the first cross promotions that I was involved with. At the time, I was part owner of a small health club that featured Nautilus® exercise equipment. After reading an article in a sports magazine about famous tennis players who used Nautilus equipment to improve their games and increase their stamina, it was quite apparent that Nautilus and tennis were made for each other.

I approached the owner of a local racquetball club with no health facilities. I showed the owner a certificate very similar to the one illustrated in Figure 2-1 and explained to him about our standard introductory membership. This membership allowed anyone to visit my club three times without any obligation for only $19.50. We figured that once they had an opportunity to experience the benefits of Nautilus training in our club, they would then want to sign up for one of our annual memberships.

I went on to explain, "I would like to offer you the opportunity of providing your members that same introductory membership at a savings of $9.75. That is half of what everyone else would pay for it. It is a great way for you to give your members a little more for their money—an added value for their membership, and a big thank you for being a member of your club. What do you think?"

He looked at me, then down at the certificate, then back at me. Barely squinting his eyes, then cocking his head ever so slightly to the left, he said, "It sounds pretty good, but how much is this going to cost me?"

"Well, let me ask you this," I responded, as if I were thinking of this off the top of my head. Then, with my voice slightly higher and with a hint of it cracking, I continued, "If it were free, would you do it?"

His eyes opened a little wider, and as if perplexed, he looked down again at the certificate and said, "I guess. Sure. Why not? What the heck?"

Figure 2-1   Cross-promotion certificate targeted for tennis players.

I extended my hand and finished with "fair enough."

Later that month, inserted in the club newsletter that was mailed to the 1000 members, was the special certificate entitling those people to the introductory membership at my club for only $9.75, with "Compliments of Wildwood Racquet Club" printed right on the piece.

Out of the 1000, 8 of them were redeemed. This was a low percentage, but let's see what the return on the investment was. First, the eight redemptions brought in $78. Then, out of those eight, one signed up for a six-month membership and five were converted to one-year memberships. The total gross sales generated from this promotion yielded $1803 in revenue on a cost of under $40, which included the printing and the typesetting.

This same basic technique has been used in various ways by many types of businesses, including restaurants, video rental stores, automotive service centers, travel agents, insurance companies, investment brokers, hair salons, and business-to-business services. Once you learn the basics of how a retail merchant cross promotion works, you can then adapt and modify it to work specifically for you. In this chapter, you will learn all of the reasons why a promotion like this gets results. Then you will begin adapting and modifying the ideas so they will work not only in your industry, but, specifically, in your local operation.

THREE Cs OF CROSS PROMOTIONS

The reason a cross promotion is effective is explained with the three Cs of cross promotion: *Cost, Control,* and *Credibility.*

· COST

There is very little cost. The expensive part about advertising is the distribution. The cost of creating a local radio, TV, or newspaper ad is relatively low compared to the cost of running that ad. With a cross promotion, however, you get free distribution of your advertising message.

When the racquet club mailed out 1000 of our special certificates, we did not have to pay for postage, stuffing, or mailing labels. To do a similar mailing on our own, even if we used the less expense third-class bulk rate instead of first-class mailing, would have cost us at least $250, and our results would have been less.

The only cost we had was for the printing of the certificates, and that cost was very little. Since it wasn't a bulk mailing or perceived as "junk mail," it wasn't necessary to use all the expensive gimmicks that junk mailers must use to get you to read their message. Usually all that is required for this type of program is black ink on color stock paper.

CONTROL

There are four types of control: *numerical, geographical, demographical,* and *competitive.*

Numerical Control

With any type of streetsmart cross promotion, you have total control over the number of certificates that you distribute. Let's say you are at a time of the year when you really need to boost sales. You want to run a very high-liability discount (very big offer) just to get customers in the door. If you go to your local newspaper or packaged coupon distributors, you have to print as many coupons as the circulation. For example, if your local paper has a circulation of 50,000, you have to distribute 50,000 coupons. You may not want that many high-liability coupons floating around.

With a cross promotion, you have total control over the numbers that go out. If you only want 5000 pieces to go out, and the local grocery store or dry cleaners has a weekly customer count of 10,000, you only give them 5000, and they pass them out only until the 5000 are gone.

Geographic Control

Most retail businesses draw the majority of their business from within a three- to five-mile radius. This radius varies depending on the type of business you run and the marketplace, but usually there is a geographical area from which you pull 80 to 90 percent of your business.

Similarly, most of the retail merchants you choose to cross promote with get their customers from a similar radius around their stores. Because you have geographic control, you can decide from which area you will pull your new customers.

For example, suppose that you are running a reasonably high volume operation and you decide to set up a promotion with the self-serve gas station next door to you. That gas station pulls the majority of its customers from roughly the same geographical area as you do. (See Figure 2-2a.) When the gas station distributes your certificates to their customers, many of them are already your customers. That means that you're discounting your regular customers, and that's money out of your pocket.

It's fine to provide a discount or added value to bring a new customer into your store and try you out for the first time, but you don't want to give a discount to a regular customer who normally pays full price.

Since cross promotions allow you geographical control, you should focus on promoting to new customers by setting up a promotion with a different gas station two miles away. Naturally, you will get fewer redemptions because the overlap of the two primary trading areas is much less (see Figure 2-2b), but the ones you do get are more likely to be *new* customers.

SOFT-SERVE SAP

Consider the promotion by a Quaker State minit-lube quick oil change unit and the Dairy Queen located right next door.

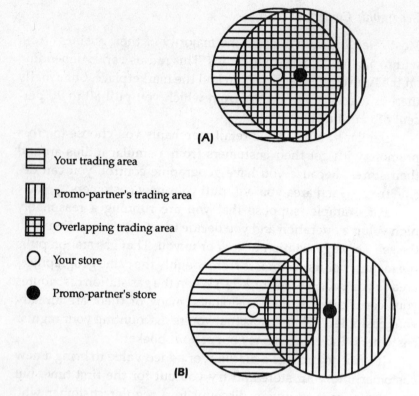

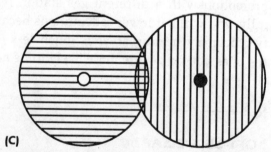

Figure 2-2 (A) Map of your primary trading area. (B) Cross-promotion partner near your location has a similar primary trading area. The overlap indicates a great deal of discounting your regular customers. (C) When your promotion is distributed further from your location, you increase your chance of getting a new customer and are less likely to discount a regular customer.

The redemption on this promotion was phenomenal. Over 70 percent were redeemed—yet this was considered a big mistake. Why? Because the vast majority of the redemptions came from minit-lube customers who brought their car in for an oil change. They had a 10 to 20 minute wait, and most of them went next door to get ice cream while they were waiting. With their purchase they got a certificate, compliments of Dairy Queen, good for $2 off at minit-lube. (See Figure 2-3.)

Figure 2-3   Tremendous redemption but at cross-purposes.

They had been ready to pay a full $20 for their oil change, but they returned with a coupon good for $2 off. If 500 coupons were redeemed, the cost would be $1000 for customers who were going to pay full price. The promotion did get a tremendous response, but was it a success? No! They may as well have displayed a stack of dollar bills for their customers to take.

When evaluating a cross promotion, don't go by the total number of redemptions. Redemptions just tell you how many people took advantage of your discount. What's more important is the number of *new* customers that come in to try you out for the first time. When evaluating your success, you must consider the regular customers who got a discount but who would normally have paid full price. That's money right out of your pocket.

You would much rather have a promotion with only 1000 redemptions if 500 of those redemptions are new customers than a promotion with 2000 redemptions and 500 new customers. Even though you would get twice as many redemptions in the second one, you would also discount 1500 of your regulars who would have paid full price.

Generally, the further away from your store you promote, the lower the number of redemptions, but of those redemptions, you get a much higher percentage of new customers.

Geographical control also allows you to pick and choose areas you want to infiltrate. You may have a major competitor two miles away. By choosing a cross promotion partner close to that competitor, you stand a very good chance of getting your competitor's customers to visit your store.

There are times of the year that may be slow for you and your regular customers forget about you for awhile. That's when to cross promote in your immediate area. That way you can get those customers back in your store before they have an opportunity to try your competition.

Some of our clients have mall locations. Geographic control for them means choosing the time to promote inside the mall and outside the mall. You may find that you're missing a great deal of business because of your location in the mall. Work that to your advantage by cross promoting with a merchant at the other end of the mall. This will bring customers down to your end.

You have the control. You can pinpoint exactly where you go. By using some strategy and a little common sense, you can get a lot of mileage out of this approach.

Demographic Control

"Demographics" refers to certain characteristics of your customers, such as age, sex, income level, education, and so on. With a cross promotion, you can choose a partner that appeals to the same type of customer that you want to attract to your store.

When we approached the racquet club to promote Nautilus, we were using demographic control. In the first chapter, the stockbroker would determine whether to pay the toll of the person behind him by the type of car that person drove. He assumed that a successful person with money to invest would be driving a Lincoln, Cadillac, Mercedes, or Rolls Royce.

You can focus on specific types of people in the same way. One example of demographic control is a sewing machine dealer who promoted with a fabric shop (see Figure 2-4). Another is an apartment complex, located within walking distance of two major hospitals, that promoted with a credit union for nurses (see Figure 2-5). Yet another promotion was a packet of certificates for a variety of merchants that all related to the wedding business. A bridal shop was using these cross-promotion certificates to help increase the value of using her shop. Her packet included special certificates for tux rental, a bakery, a photographer, entertainment, a florist, a hair salon, a banquet hall, and so on.

Demographic control plays a more important role when your type of business is not focused on a geographical neighborhood. Stockbrokers, insurance agents, office equipment stores, and lawn care services are examples in which location is not as important as the type of people who buy the products and services.

You can use demographic control to focus on the type of people that you want. Those people most likely to use a lawn care

Figure 2-4   Promotion for a very narrow target audience.

service might also need their houses painted, home improvements, or swimming pool maintenance. Or, using a combination of demographic and geographic control, you can focus on more affluent neighborhoods by promoting with retail merchants in that area.

An office equipment store could cross promote with other businesses or with organizations that serve businesses such as the local Chamber of Commerce, temporary-help services, banks, agencies that sell business insurance, and uniform shops. The idea is to find businesses that have customers who could potentially be your customers as well. Then cross promote with those businesses.

Competitive Control

When you place your ad in the local newspaper or on the local radio or TV station, your competition knows exactly what you're

Compliments of MedPAC

ONE MONTH FREE RENT

The bearer of this certificate is a member of the MedPAC Federal Credit Union and is entitled to one month free rent at Colonial Apartments, when signing a twelve month lease at the regular price. Not combinable with any other discount or special. Offer expires August 15 1982. Only one certificate per apartment.

For information call
483-2022
East State at Hobson

One, Two, & Three
Bedroom Apartments
Available

Figure 2-5   This promotion saved thousands of dollars by protecting the regular price credibility. Also a good example of targeting a narrow audience.

doing, and they can react. But with a cross promotion, your competition has no idea what's going on. They may be aware of one cross promotion that you've done with one merchant, and a couple of months later they may see something else you've done. They have no idea that you're actually systematically defining and defending your turf. By the time they figure out what's really going on, it's too late. You own your turf.

CREDIBILITY

The last of the three Cs is credibility. This is rapidly becoming the most important feature of successful cross promotions. One of the biggest problems facing most businesses is that there is too much discounting and couponing. Customers have been conditioned to expect a deal every time they walk in the door. This is a very serious problem that is eroding profit margins.

The published price means nothing anymore. The last time you bought a car, you no doubt were able to negotiate money off the sticker price. Why? Car dealers have conditioned you to come in and haggle over price. Then the car manufacturers became very aggressive by offering extra incentives: free options, cash back, and low financing. It's effective in boosting sales on a short-term basis, but if this is done over a long period of time, consumers will wait for the next announcement of special incentives before they buy.

The airlines have done the same with their frequent flier programs. At first, it proved to be a great way to build loyalty. It is a powerful program. Yet, when things become competitive, there is a bonus mileage war. At this writing, all of the airlines have come out with triple miles. As a result, some paying customers are getting bumped from flights, and it's costing the airlines a great deal of money. To compensate, they raise prices to pay for all the trips they're giving away free.

Department stores have done the same thing. You have, no doubt, watched people shop in department stores. They spend hours finding exactly what they want. Then the first thing they say to the sales clerk is, "When does this go on sale?"

Some department stores have sales at the end of every month. They're appropriately called EOM (End of the Month). Who would buy anything in the middle of the month when they know that the price will be slashed in just a couple of weeks? And while they are waiting for it to go on sale, perhaps they will find something else they like better at another store or just realize that they really could live without it.

Sales are effective, yet the more sales you have, the more your regular-price credibility suffers.

THE COUPOHOLIC

Excessive mass coupons are just as dangerous to your regular-price credibility. When things get tough, businesses roll out the coupons. Large companies will mail out coupons to your house. They insert coupons in the newspaper. They group mail coupons with mass-mailing companies. They even have people on street corners handing them out. Coupons are found everywhere. Businesses who are addicted to coupons as a primary marketing tool are what I call "coupoholics."

It starts out innocently enough. Sales drop during a slow season and the Val-Pak sales representative drops off some literature. The price looks good, so you go with it. Ten thousand households in your neighborhood get your coupon. It works. Customers come in. Redemption is good and sales go up.

Next week the community tabloid has a special. They'll throw in a second color free. You run a coupon. It works. You get some more sales. Then you do a mailing of your own with a series of coupons. You get some more sales. Before you know it, you're running a coupon several times a month. You're hooked. Soon your customers ask you when you're running your next coupon. They wait. They only buy from you with a coupon. Now they're hooked.

MARKETING METHODONE

Done properly, coupons can be an effective way to introduce your business to new customers. However, if you continue to coupon your regular customers, they become conditioned to expect a deal every time they walk in the store.

I was having lunch one day at a restaurant next to another fast-food chain and heard a couple say, "We were going to go next door, but we forgot our coupons!"

The next time I went into the restaurant they spoke of, the coupon idea was reinforced. The counterperson did *not* say, "It's good to see you, what can I get for you?" I was *not* asked, "Would you like to try our brand new sandwich? It's really wonderful." Instead, the first thing I was asked was, "Do you have any coupons today?"

That person just informed me that everyone else in the world is paying less money than I am. One particular fast food restaurant I go to does it even better. They don't ask, "Do you have any coupons today?" They ask, "*Which* coupon do you have today?!"

Sometimes I just can't help myself. I hear them ask that question and it makes me angry. Without thinking, I respond,

"No, I don't have any coupons today. How much did I get taken for?"

When coupons are overused, the menu board behind the counter with the prices has absolutely no credibility. It means nothing because most of the customers know they can get a discount with a coupon.

In our town, a certain pizza chain started a delivery service. This one does theirs a little differently. Instead of calling the specific location that services your area, you need only call one central number and the order is dispatched. You call up and the first thing they ask you is not your name, but your telephone number. You give it to them, and they come back with something like, "Mr. Slutsky at 34 West Whittier. How are you today? Last time you ordered on June 10th at 12:04 P.M. It was a small mushroom and onion with extra cheese. Would you like the same again?"

I give them my order. Then the order taker asks me that one fatal question: "Do you have any coupons?"

This time I am prepared. I ask, "Do you take other people's coupons?"

"Oh, sure. We'll take anybody's!" she says proudly.

"Great! I have one from minit-lube."

They took it! I couldn't believe it, but they did take it. The delivery guy came to our office and handed me the pizza. I gave him my coupon for $2 off on an oil change, and he took $2 off the bill.

This pizza chain, however, totally lost its price credibility with me. I have no reason ever to pay full price.

If a business is willing to discount that easily, or to accept anyone's coupons without so much as a glance, you really have to wonder how this effects the mind-set of the buying public.

CAR WASH WOES

One of the most extreme cases of coupoholism was when I went to get my car washed at a full-service car wash that I visit with some degree of frequency. I really like to go to this particular car wash because they do a super job, not because they offer a deal. My favorite part is at the end. They have what seems like 14 guys drying off my car. What attention. I feel like a million bucks when I get my car washed there.

Once I went there on a Tuesday. This must have been the first time I ever visited them on a Tuesday because, as soon as I pulled up, the attendant asked me if I had my Tuesday 99¢ coupon. I informed him that I didn't. He then persisted, "Gee, this is Tuesday. It's coupon day. Everyone brings their coupon with them on Tuesday."

"I understand, but unfortunately I do not have a coupon; I'm sure your boss won't mind if I pay full price."

"I hate to see you not have a coupon on coupon day. There's a newsstand just a couple blocks away, and if you got a paper you could cut out our coupon and use it."

By now I'm getting a little upset. "Listen, I don't mind paying full price. I'm in a hurry and I just want to get my car washed. I'm going to give you the full $5.00 for a car wash and I'm going to give you another $5.00 to shut up and let me go!"

I'll never go back there without my coupon. I might not go back there at all, but if I do, it will be on Tuesday. I don't really need to save the money on the wash, but I don't want to feel like I'm getting ripped off by paying full price. I didn't go there because I could save money, but rather because I liked the quality of the service. That was totally destroyed by one attendant who couldn't understand that.

PROTECTING YOUR PRICE CREDIBILITY

A cross promotion allows you to use an incentive, such as a discount, an added value, or a premium gift, and at the same time protect your price credibility. You protect your price credibility by transferring the responsibility to someone else.

When my health club was able to get the racquet club to distribute our 50 percent off introductory membership offer to it's members, Nautilus wasn't giving up a discount. On the actual certificate (Figure 2-1), it says, "compliments of Wildwood." It gives the impression that the racquet club is totally responsible for arranging this special deal on behalf of its members. In that way, six racquet club members signed up for full memberships without asking for a discount or a deal. We protected our price credibility.

A good example of protecting your price credibility is the story about the "one-month free rent" (Figure 2-5). This particular property was in a slump, as was the entire market. Many other properties were advertising in media such as the newspaper, radio, and even on billboards. They said that you could get one month free with a year lease. Some were so desperate that they offered two months free with a year lease. This was a very powerful promotion because it would save the potential tenant a great deal of money. In this particular market, the savings would be $350 to $550 or more.

However, there was a big problem with the promotion that most property managers did not anticipate. Let's say that your apartment complex has 500 units. You're renting 80 percent of them when you're used to renting around 95 percent. Even though you are down to only 80 percent, you still have 400 people paying you between $350 to $550 rent every month. At any one time, you may have 30 or more of your paying tenants up for a lease renewal. They see your ad for "one month free with a year lease." They come to the office to discuss renewing their lease, and guess what they ask for?

Now you are in a difficult situation. Some managers calmly explain that this offer is only for new leases, because they have to hit a certain level of occupancy before the manager can get a bonus. Naturally, your existing tenant, who has been paying you $425 every month, is very understanding and willing to help you out.

Then there is the real world.

Either you give them the free month which costs you $425, or you refuse and stand the possiblity of losing that tenant to one of your competitors who is more than happy to extend the offer, and that will cost you $5100.

We took a different approach. We used the mass media (primarily classified advertising in the local newspaper) to advertise the benefits to our potential renters. "Spacious rooms. Great location. No rats." Then we used cross promotions to make the same offer to a select group of people.

In this particular example, we networked with a federal credit union that serves 3300 nurses. Since this property is located within walking distance of two major hospitals, it made sense to go after the nurses' credit union. This was just one of many promotions that this credit union did.

As a result of this particular approach, the majority of the existing tenants who were up for renewal did not know about the promotion, and, therefore, they didn't feel cheated when it wasn't offered to them. Even those that did find out about the promotion didn't feel cheated. They knew they didn't qualify because they did not belong to that credit union.

There was one nurse who received the certificate and whose lease was up for renewal. Of course, her certificate was honored. Even so, the savings for the month was over $12,000! Protecting your price credibility saves you a lot of money as well as headaches.

Notice that in all the examples given, the certificate always includes a "compliments of," with the cross-promotion partner's company name and/or logo. In some promotions, we even put the name of the manager as well as the company logo. This transfers the responsibility twice as much, plus it is an added bonus for the manager. He or she has probably never seen his or her name printed ten thousand times before. This can be a boost to the ego, and as a consequence, they'll make sure that each of their customers gets one of the thank-you certificates.

If you really want to stroke your partner, use a signature (Figure 2-6). Be sure to get the signature on white paper using a

Compliments of the
Delaware Area Chamber of Commerce

VALUE CARD

The bearer of this card is affiliated with:

and is entitled to one **FREE LARGE ORDER OF FRENCH FRIES** with the purchase of any large sandwich* at the regular price. Valid only at **McDonald's® of Delaware, 279 S. Sandusky or 2091 US 23 North. Show your card at time of purchase. Expires: 6/30/86**

Not valid with any other offer. Limit one card per person per purchase. Cash value 1/20th of 1¢. *(Big Mac* Sandwich, †Quarter Pounder, or †Quarter Pounder with Cheese Sandwich, (†weight before cooking 113.4 gms.), Chicken McNuggets* , or McD.L.T.*)
1986 McDonald's Corporation

Compliments of the
Delaware Area Chamber of Commerce

VALUE CARD

The bearer of this card is affiliated with:

and is entitled to one **FREE LARGE ORDER OF FRENCH FRIES** with the purchase of any large sandwich* at the regular price. Valid only at **McDonald's® of Delaware, 279 S. Sandusky or 2091 US 23 North. Show your card at time of purchase. Expires: 6/30/86**

Not valid with any other offer. Limit one card per person per purchase. Cash value 1/20th of 1¢. *(Big Mac* Sandwich, †Quarter Pounder, or †Quarter Pounder with Cheese Sandwich, (†weight before cooking 113.4 gms.), Chicken McNuggets* , or McD.L.T.*)
1986 McDonald's Corporation

Compliments of the
Delaware Area Chamber of Commerce

VALUE CARD

The bearer of this card is affiliated with:

and is entitled to one **FREE LARGE ORDER OF FRENCH FRIES** with the purchase of any large sandwich* at the regular price. Valid only at **McDonald's® of Delaware, 279 S. Sandusky or 2091 US 23 North. Show your card at time of purchase. Expires: 6/30/86**

Not valid with any other offer. Limit one card per person per purchase. Cash value 1/20th of 1¢. *(Big Mac* Sandwich, †Quarter Pounder, or †Quarter Pounder with Cheese Sandwich, (†weight before cooking 113.4 gms.), Chicken McNuggets* , or McD.L.T.*)
1986 McDonald's Corporation

Compliments of the
Delaware Area Chamber of Commerce

VALUE CARD

The bearer of this card is affiliated with:

and is entitled to one **FREE LARGE ORDER OF FRENCH FRIES** with the purchase of any large sandwich* at the regular price. Valid only at **McDonald's® of Delaware, 279 S. Sandusky or 2091 US 23 North. Show your card at time of purchase. Expires: 6/30/86**

Not valid with any other offer. Limit one card per person per purchase. Cash value 1/20th of 1¢. *(Big Mac* Sandwich, †Quarter Pounder, or †Quarter Pounder with Cheese Sandwich, (†weight before cooking 113.4 gms.), Chicken McNuggets* , or McD.L.T.*)
1986 McDonald's Corporation

Compliments of the
Delaware Area Chamber of Commerce

VALUE CARD

The bearer of this card is affiliated with:

and is entitled to one **FREE LARGE ORDER OF FRENCH FRIES** with the purchase of any large sandwich* at the regular price. Valid only at **McDonald's® of Delaware, 279 S. Sandusky or 2091 US 23 North. Show your card at time of purchase. Expires: 6/30/86**

Not valid with any other offer. Limit one card per person per purchase. Cash value 1/20th of 1¢. *(Big Mac* Sandwich, †Quarter Pounder, or †Quarter Pounder with Cheese Sandwich, (†weight before cooking 113.4 gms.), Chicken McNuggets* , or McD.L.T.*)
1986 McDonald's Corporation

Compliments of the
Delaware Area Chamber of Commerce

VALUE CARD

The bearer of this card is affiliated with:

and is entitled to one **FREE LARGE ORDER OF FRENCH FRIES** with the purchase of any large sandwich* at the regular price. Valid only at **McDonald's® of Delaware, 279 S. Sandusky or 2091 US 23 North. Show your card at time of purchase. Expires: 6/30/86**

Not valid with any other offer. Limit one card per person per purchase. Cash value 1/20th of 1¢. *(Big Mac* Sandwich, †Quarter Pounder, or †Quarter Pounder with Cheese Sandwich, (†weight before cooking113.4 gms.), Chicken McNuggets* , or McD.L.T.*)
1986 McDonald's Corporation

Dear Chamber Member:

Here's an exciting employee benefit program that won't cost you a cent!

For the next 90 days, every time one of your employees visits McDonald's® of Delaware (279 S. Sandusky or 2091 US 23 North), by merely presenting their Special Employee Value Card they'll receive one **FREE LARGE ORDER OF FRENCH FRIES** with the purchase of any large sandwich*.

Your employees can use these cards over and over again over the next three months!

All you have to do is have someone type or write in the name of your business on the cards and distribute them to your employees. If you have more than 12 employees, call us here at the Chamber at 369-6221 for additional cards. Do it today! So your employees can get the full benefits of this exciting three month program!

Sincerely,

Marcus J. Molea, AICP
Executive Manager
Delaware Area Chamber
of Commerce

(Big Mac Sandwich, *Quarter Pounder, or *Quarter Pounder with Cheese Sandwich, (weight before cooking 113.4 gms.), Chicken McNuggets* , or McD.L.T.*)
©1986 McDonald's Corporation

Figure 2-6 A hand signature adds a personal touch to a cross promotion.

Compliments of Turk Johnson

TWO FOR ONE ON MONDAY

This coupon entitles the bearer to receive two drinks for
the price of one any Monday from 3 p.m. to 1 a.m.
Cannot be combined with any other discount.
Only one coupon per person.
Expires September 30, 1981

Compliments of Brickley's Fire House

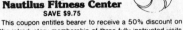

**All Sports
Nautilus Fitness Center**
SAVE $9.75

This coupon entitles bearer to receive a 50% discount on
the introductory membership of three fully instructed visits.
Regular price is $19.75.

**On South Calhoun across from South Side.
Call for appointment 456-1956**
Only one per person. Expires September 30, 1981.

Compliments of Brickley's Fire House

FREE FRENCH FRIES

with the purchase of any sandwich
at regular price (excludes junior)

Good after 10:00 p.m.

Good only at Arby's at Rudisill

Expires September 30, 1981

Compliments of Brickley's Fire House

 PIZZA KING

BUY ONE PIZZA, GET THE 2nd SAME
SIZE PIZZA FOR HALF PRICE.
GOOD MONDAY THRU THURSDAY
DINING ROOM OR CARRY OUT

Offer valid with coupon only. One coupon per customer. Not good in combination with
other offers, coupons, or discounts. Expires October 15, 1981

Compliments of Brickley's Fire House

20th Century Automotive

OIL CHANGE FOR ONLY $14⁹⁵

This coupon entitles bearer to receive an oil change for
only $14.95, a savings of over $5.00. Only one coupon
per person. Cannot be combined with any other discount.

Call for appointment 432-5325 • 1001 Leesburg Road
"If we can't fix it, it can't be fixed!"
Expires September 30, 1981

Compliments of B. J. Holiday

 Brickley's Fire House
AFTER WORK SPECIAL
TWO FOR ONE

This coupon entitles bearer to receive two drinks for
the price of one any day between 3 p.m. and 6 p.m.
Only one coupon per person.
Cannot be combined with any other discount.
Expires September 30, 1981.

Compliments of Steve Diamond

**WQHK
OLDIES NIGHT
PRIMER**

With Rick Hughes • **Free Mixed Drink**
This coupon entitles the bearer to a free mixed drink when
purchased the same drink at the regular price.
Good only Thursday between 7:00 p.m. and 8:30 p.m.
Cannot be combined with any other discount.
Only one coupon per person. Expires 9/30/81.

Compliments of Brickley's Fire House

THREE PIECE CHICKEN DINNER
Mashed Potatoes, Cole Slaw & Biscuit

SAVE 50¢ • ONLY $2.05

Good at any Fort Wayne location
Expires September 30, 1981

Figure 2-7 This reverse cross promotion was used not only as an added
value, but to these neighboring merchants happy enough to allow the use of
their parking lots after hours.

45

black pen or felt-tip marker. Don't use blue because it does not reproduce well.

The ultimate stroking is done by putting the manager's picture right on the piece. This works particularly well when you're dealing with a union president who is up for re-election soon.

Even when you do a bounce-back or in-house certificate, you will still want to transfer the responsibility to someone else. In the nightclub I once owned, we had a special promotion that ran for six weeks. We featured male dancers on Monday nights. It packed the place on the night that we normally would have been closed because it was so slow. Even so, most of the women attending this special promotion on Monday were not our regular customers later in the week, so we wanted to provide them a special incentive to return.

At the door, with their paid cover, they received a multiple cross-promotion piece that included savings from neighborhood establishments as well as discounts for later in the week at the nightclub. (The liquor laws have become much stricter since this promotion.) On the internal certificates, we transferred the responsibility of the discount to the men on stage, as if to thank their audience for their attendance.

By the way, this particular cross promotion is referred to as a reverse cross promotion because we included special deals to be given away at our door. (See Figure 2-7.) We, in effect, helped our neighborhood businesses advertise to our customers for free. In addition to providing our customers with added value (at no cost to us except for printing), we established a wonderful rapport with our business neighbors; they happily allowed us to use their parking lots after 6:00 P.M.

CUSTOMIZE TO YOU

The next step, and perhaps the most important, is to customize this concept for your own business. You have read about a number of different types of businesses that have used cross promotions, but the key is to figure out how to adapt, modify, and improve them to work for you.

◇ People Magnet Exercise

This exercise helps. Take a sheet of lined paper and at the top, write "People Magnet Exercise." Then number the lines 1 through 25. Next, write down 25 different types of "people magnets" that make sense for your type of operation. A "people magnet" is a place that attracts the same type of people that you want as customers. In this particular exercise, only concern yourself with retail merchants. There are other techniques that are designed to work specifically with major employers, associations, and nonprofit groups.

The narrower your target audience, the more difficult this exercise becomes and the more important it is to be selective. For example, when we worked with a sewing machine company, we knew that only a small percentage of the population bought sewing machines. It wouldn't make sense to do cross promotions with mass-appeal type businesses such as a grocery store or a fast-food restaurant because, even though you would get a great deal of exposure, the chances of your getting your promotional piece into the hands of a potential sewing machine buyer is very low. Instead, we worked with fabric shops, hobby shops, shoe stores, and even sewing clubs.

On the other hand, if your business does have mass appeal, such as an auto service center, a restaurant, or a hair salon, then it is fine to do cross promotions with other businesses of this type. In this case, you will want to find those businesses that appeal to the vast majority of the population on a regular basis. The following are examples of people magnets that you may want to include in your list:

Dry Cleaner	Rust Proofing	Office Supply
Restaurant	Quick Oil Change	Car Dealership

Car Wash	Printer	Appliance Store
Department Store	Toy Store	Furniture Store
Gas Station	Optical	Tire Store
Grocery Store	Diet Center	Ice Cream/Yogurt
Convenience Store	Health Club	Motel/Hotel
Bank/Savings & Loan	Drug Store	Car Rental
Video Rental	Roller Skating Rink	Airline
Photo Processing	Bowling Alley	Shoe Store
Apartment Complex	Movie Theatre	Record Store
Home Center	Lawn & Garden Service	Amusement Park
Clothing Store	Home Security	Paint Store

These are just some examples; there are many others. It's important that you include in your list only those that make sense for you. You also must be aware of whether a type of business on your list feels that you are a competitor. Sometimes grocery stores that have delicatessens won't work with restaurants. A long-distance telephone company may consider a greeting card company to be a major competitor. Of course it never hurts to ask, but be aware of what potential problems you may have.

Continuing with the exercise, you will now customize it for an individual store. Remember, to be effective, streetsmart marketing is executed on the local level by the local owner-operator or manager—the person with whom your customers have daily contact.

If you are in a supervisory position, and your responsibility is to work with a number of stores, choose one of your stores that you're most familiar with and use that for the purpose of this exercise.

◇ Neighborhood Merchant Cross-Promotion Exercise

Part One—Write at the top of another piece of ruled paper, "Neighborhood Merchant Certificate Exercise." Then number your paper from 1 to 10. List 10 neighborhood merchants who you think would make good cross-promotion partners for your store or business. If you have multiple locations, have your managers do this exercise. Do one for each location. Write the actual business name. If, for example, you think it would be beneficial to cross promote with Jeff's Car Wash three blocks away, write down "Jeff's Car Wash." Use the 25 people magnets as a guide for the type of local merchants you're looking for.

Part Two—Now go back through your list of 10. If you know the owner, manager, or an employee who has some influence at the store, circle the number. For example, if you wrote "Jeff's Car Wash" under #3, and you happen to know Jeff, then circle #3. You don't have to be best buddies with Jeff, but should know him well enough to say "hi" if you passed each other at the mall.

Part Three—Go back one more time through your list. This time, place an "X" in the margin to the left of each of the 10 businesses in which the owner, manager, or influential employee is a customer of yours. You'll probably have some overlap between those numbers you've circled and those that have an "X."

EASY DOES IT

The reason for this exercise is simple. When I first started teaching this program in seminars all around the country, one of the most frequent comments I received from my attendees in the evaluations was, "Jeff, this stuff is really great, but I'm already working 65 hours a week. I just don't have time to go knocking on doors."

This is a valid comment. I would then ask them how much time they felt they could realistically devote to their streetfighting efforts if they knew that their efforts would pay off in increased sales. The response was usually a couple of hours a week.

That's all the time you really need. In the beginning stages, when you're first learning, it does take more time, but we've found that if you stick with it for one month, or two at the most, you can develop and maintain your streetfighting program in less than two hours a week if you do it on a steady basis. Furthermore, you can incorporate these efforts right into your business. In most cases, all it takes is about five minutes here and ten minutes there.

This is just the first of many such exercises. To get the most out this program, you must do them. Each of your managers must do them. By the time you're finished with the first half of this book, you will have a complete plan for a customized streetfighting program, with over a hundred promotions placed in priority and geared specifically for each of your stores.

CROSS-PROMOTION VARIATIONS

REVERSE

We've already discussed the reverse cross promotion. As you recall, this is when you get certificates from other businesses to pass out to your customers. One of the more interesting reverse promotions was used by a bridal shop as a closing technique to get future brides to have this shop do their weddings.

She contacted a number of different merchants whose businesses could be related to weddings. These included a photographer, a florist, a formalwear store, a printer, a mobile disco, a jeweler, a caterer, a banquet hall, a hair salon, a diet clinic, and an apartment complex.

All of the certificates were printed on separate cards that looked like a wedding invitation. They were then placed in a nice envelope. The total value of the package, if redeemed, was over

$500. This was not only a nice savings, but was also a great aid in planning the wedding.

2-WAY

The 2-way is a little easier to set up because the benefits for passing out your promotion pieces is more readily understood. The negative aspect of this is that it creates more work for you. I don't mind doing a 2-way once in awhile, but I certainly don't want to work a 2-way with every promotion that I do.

Another advantage of the 2-way is that you do not necessarily have to provide a value in your piece. In the Skippers/minitlube example, Skippers used their piece to create additional awareness for a TV campaign that they were running. The piece itself does not have a value attached to it.

A more elaborate 2-way cross promotion involved AT&T Phone Centers and Chick-fil-A. This was done in a number of states in the Southwest. At Chick-fil-A, customers registered to win a free AT&T telephone. The entry form required name, address, phone number, and the question, "Do you use AT&T long distance on your home telephone?" From this information, AT&T developed a mailing/telemarketing list for follow-up promotions.

Both of these merchants are located in major malls. At the AT&T location, usually on the other side of the mall from Chick-fil-A, coupons were given free with a purchase. These were good for a free sandwich at Chick-fil-A. Counter and salespeople at both stores wore special buttons and visors that promoted these offers. (See Figure 2-8.)

The bigger 2-way promotions can even incorporate mass media advertising. This happened several years ago when Arby's and Baskin Robbins in Chicago teamed up. Both ran a mass-media campaign announcing the availability of special certificates for a free Arby's sandwich with an ice cream purchase at Baskin Robbins, and vice versa. In this way, both organizations used their respective offers as an added value as well as a way to get more mileage out of their mass-media dollars.

WIN

A QUALITY AT&T TELEPHONE

Fill out this form and drop it into the ballot box located in this store. The drawing will be held June 1, 1987. You do not have to be present to win. No purchase necessary to register.

Name _____

Address _____

City, State, Zip _____

Phone No. _____

Do you now use **AT&T** long distance on your home phone?   ☐ YES ☐ NO
Must be 18 or older to enter.

Thank you for your **AT&T** purchase. Redeem this coupon for a FREE Chick-fil-A Sandwich at your nearest participating Chick-fil-A restaurant with this coupon.

Closed Sundays. Coupon not good with any other offer.
Exp. 6-13-87

 Spring Forward with **AT&T** and Chick-fil-A

 Spring Forward with **AT&T** and Chick-fil-A

REGISTER TO WIN A QUALITY AT&T TELEPHONE

1–You must be 18 years or older to enter.
2–No purchase necessary.
3–You do not have to be present to win.
4–Contest ends May 31, 1987. Drawing will be held June 1st, 1987.

Spring Forward with **AT&T** and Chick-fil-A

Figure 2-8   2-way with free drawing.

REIMBURSABLE CROSS PROMOTION

Another cross promotion involves getting your cross-promotion partner to pay for your certificates. This is an advanced technique, and you certainly should not start out doing it, but it is something to keep in mind.

The Chick-fil-A philosophy is to give a sandwich away the first time. This is because they know they have an excellent product, and that once it is sampled, they will have a loyal customer. So, instead of a discount, Chick-fil-A usually distributes a free sandwich card called a BOG ("Be Our Guest").

This is a very strong approach because the offer is powerful and it keeps you out of the discount pasture. If you offer a discount coupon, your customers might expect coupons all of the time, but with a freebie, they know it's a one-time special offer.

One restaurant operator offered to provide one of the nations leading department stores credit managers BOG cards at 99¢ each. The sandwich sells for around $1.85. Then he suggested that the BOG cards be used as in incentive for people to fill out the department store credit card application.

The department store bought 500 to start. Think about this! The department store paid just under $500 and distributed the restaurant's advertising for free. Yet, the department store gave its customers a strong incentive to fill out that credit application. Everybody won!

By the time the promotion had ended, the department store bought a total of 10,000 Chick-fil-A BOGs!

VALUE CARD

The value card is a format that allows you to infiltrate many areas that you might not be able to get into with the standard cross-promotion certificate. The value card is usually a special deal that the customers can use over and over again for a certain period of time. This is usually 60 or 90 days in most retail establishments. Since you are giving the customers a savings or added value each time they come into your store, you can usually offer a lesser value than you would if it were a one-time savings offered through a standard cross-promotion certificate.

The long form of the value card (Figure 2-9) offers the recipient a good explanation of the program. The top part is detached and discarded, and the smaller part is kept in the customer's wallet or purse. This is important because your advertising message is kept with them at all times. It is a constant reminder that you are there to serve them.

The merchant-certificate cross promotion works best with neighborhood merchants. The value card format works best when dealing with major employers, associations and/or organizations, and educational institutions. Many of these larger businesses find that the standard merchant certificate is too commercial; however, they're accustomed to working with VIP or ID cards.

Between the two formats, the merchant certificate is the best for you because it gets the customers in your store. Then it's your job to make sure the customer is happy and will keep coming back. (Required reading for help in this area is *How to Win Customers and Keep Them for Life,* by Dr. Michael LeBoeuf.) But if it's a choice between having a value card or no promotion at all, you'll want to take the value card every time.

In the early days of streetfighting, we called these "discount cards." But in recent years, the word "discount" has assumed a negative connotation when it comes to setting up the promotions. It gives a potential cross-promotion partner a subtle feeling that you're trying to put one over him, but by referring to them as value cards, there is less resistance.

WHEN TO WALK

When talking to major employers in your community, you may find that they want to do the promotion, but that they don't

Dear Member:

We recently arranged with Carpetland USA for complimentary 10% discount cards.

With this card you will receive a 10% discount on any non-commercial carpet and vinyl floor covering in stock. Sale merchandise is also included!

This card may be used over and over again for as long as indicated by the expiration date below. Please note that the card does not apply to special orders or installation.

Carpetland USA reserves the right to ask for identification to prove your affiliation with us.

If you have any questions, call Carpetland USA at 489—4584.

DISCOUNT CARD   1111 W. Washington Ctr. Rd. (219) 489—4584

The bearer of this card is affiliated with:

Allen County Postal Employees Credit Union

and is entitled to a 10% discount on all non-commercial carpet and vinyl floor covering in stock. Cannot be combined with any other discount or special. Only one card per person per purchase.
EXPIRES: FEB 1983

WESTERN AUTO

Dear Employee:

Recently, we arranged with McDonald's® of Delaware on 279 S. Sandusky for you to get your own McDonald's Special Value Card.

With this special card you will receive one free Large Order of French Fries with the purchase of any large sandwich*. Simply detach the card below and present it at the time of purchase.

Your Special Value Card can be used over and over again for as long as indicated by the expiration date below. Please note this special arrangement is not valid with any other special or coupon and subject to the terms and conditions stated below on your card.

Your Special Value Card is provided specifically for your use only. McDonald's reserves the right to ask for identification to prove your affiliation with us.

We're very pleased to provide you this extra benefit, so feel free to start using it right away. And remember, "It's A Good Time, For The Great Taste®", of McDonald's!*.

LC

VALUE CARD
The bearer of this card is affiliated with:
WESTERN AUTO

and is entitled to one FREE LARGE ORDER OF FRENCH FRIES with the purchase of any large sandwich* at the regular price. Valid only at McDonald's® at 279 S. Sandusky, Delaware Ohio. Show your card at time of purchase. Expires: 7/30/86.

Not valid with any other offer. Limit one card per person per purchase. Cash value
*"Big Mac" Sandwich, †Quarter Pounder, or †Quarter Pounder with Cheese Sandwich. (†weight before cooking 113.4 grms.), Chicken McNuggets®, or McD.L.T.®)
© 1986 McDonald's Corporation

RAINIER BANK®

Dear Employee:

Recently, we arranged with the Minit-Lube® located at:

10022 Holman Rd. N.W.
(corner of 3rd & 100th N.W.)

for you to get your own special Minit-Lube Value Card. With your Special Value Card you will save $2.00 on the regular price of full service lubrication featuring Quaker State products. Simply detach the card below and present it at the time of purchase.

Your Special Value Card can be used over and over again for as long as indicated by the expiration date below. Please note that special arrangement is not valid in combination with any other offer and subject to the terms and conditions stated on your card.

Your Special Value Card is provided specifically for your use only. Minit-Lube reserves the right to ask for identification to prove your affiliation with us.

We're very pleased to provide you this extra benefit so feel free to start using it right away. And remember to "look for the Stripes®".

minit-lube®
VALUE CARD
the bearer of this card is affiliated with
RAINIER BANK
and is entitled to a $2 savings on the regular price of the full service lubrication. valid only at 10022 Holman Rd. N.W.

We feature Quaker State products

Not valid in combination with any other offer. Limit one card per person per visit.
No Appointment Necessary.   Expires: 12/31/86.

Figure 2-9   Value cards to infiltrate major employers.

want to distribute the pieces to their employees. They'll tell you that they'll put an announcement in their newsletter, and anyone who wants one can pick it up at the office. If that is the only way you can get distribution, then walk away from the promotion; you would just be wasting your time. You would get no new customers, and you would only end up discounting your regular ones who are already willing to pay full price. The only ones that will bother to pick them up are your regulars.

The magic of these promotions is that you get the advertising message in the hands of potential customers. They have to handle it, see it, and deal with it. At least you can make some kind of impression on the way to the wastebasket, if that is where it's headed. However, if the employer, organization, or institution feels strongly enough about providing their people with an extra benefit, then the recipients are more likely to react positively to it as well. You will learn how to deal with this situation, as well as how to set up a promotion, in the next chapter.

Once you set up the artwork for your value card, the only thing that changes is the logo or name of the partner in the top portion, the name of the organization in the card portion, and the expiration date. Also, make sure that your salutation is correct. Use "Dear members" if it is a member; use "Dear employee" if you are dealing with a major employer; use "Dear student" if your partner is an educational institution.

◇ Value Card Exercise

Part One—At the top of a sheet of paper, write "Value Card Exercises." Next, write "Major Employers," and number from 1 to 5. After that, write "Associations/Organizations," and number from 1 to 5. Last, write "Educational Institutions," and number from 1 to 5.

Your exercise is to write down specific partners who would best be served by using the value card approach. List

five major employers in your area, five major associati[on]
or organizations, and five educational institutions.

A major employer can be any business that has from a few
hundred employees up to tens of thousands. It all depends on
your particular community. Associations can include groups
such as unions, credit unions, trade associations, and so on.
Educational institutions can be major colleges or universities,
but you'll probably find it very difficult to get a major university
to work with you on a campus-wide basis. Your best bet would
be to break the university down into smaller, more accessible
groups, such as various student committees or clubs, fraterni-
ties and sororities, the dormitories, and so on. You can also
work with the smaller institutions, such as technical and voca-
tional schools, beauty schools, or truck driving schools. Look
around your community and you will begin to see all of the
opportunities that are there.

Part Two—Now go back through your list of 15. If you
know the owner or other decision maker, such as the president,
personnel director, or manager, circle the number.

Part Three—Go back through your list one more time.
This time place an "X" next to each one of the 15 in which the
key person is a customer of yours. You'll probably have some
overlap between those numbers you've circled and those that
receive the "X."

Helpful Hint—If you're not familiar with your area, take
some time to explore. Perhaps you could take a different way to
and from work for a couple of weeks. Get to know what is going
on in your area. Know your turf. By the time you are finished
with the first half of this book, you'll know numerous ways to
tap into the countless opportunities for free exposure that are
in your area.

12-IN-1

The next variation of the value card allows you to get 12 times
the normal distribution of the standard value card; however, it is

a limited application. The 12-in-1 value card is used exclusively by businesses or organizations who serve other businesses. (See Figure 2-6 and 2-10.)

The 12-in-1 is distributed to the owner or manager of a small business in your community by a business or organization that serves other businesses. Some business-to-business people magnets include:

Better Business Bureau	Small Business Administration
Downtown Merchants Association	Mall Merchants Association
Office Supply	Office Furniture
Quick Printer	Cash Register Company
Security Services	Power Company
Advertising Media	Window Washers/Maintenance
Sanitation	Construction Companies
Consulting Companies	Computer Stores/Consultants
Temporary Labor Services	Employment Agencies
Auto/Fleet Leasing	Car Phone Sales
Bank	Trash Removal
Telecommunications	Pagers

The difference between these types of people magnets and all of the others is these types of businesses and organizations have the ability to provide not only the owner or manager with a value card for him or herself, but to distribute a value card to each of the employees in that organization.

The instructions in our fast-food example read:

Dear Chamber Member:

Here's an exciting employee benefit program that won't cost you a cent. For the next 90 days, every time one of your employees visits the [Name of Restaurant] by merely presenting their Special Employee Value Card, they'll receive one FREE LARGE ORDER OF FRENCH FRIES with the purchase of any large sandwich.

Your employees can use these cards over and over again for the next three months. All you have to do is have someone

THE NO-HASSLE LUBE & OIL SERVICE.

(Quaker State® Minit-Lube, 1988

(insert address, bold)

DEAR CHAMBER MEMBER:

We have made a special arrangement for an exciting employee benefit program that won't cost you a cent!

For the next six months, every time you or one of your employees visits the Minit-Lube locations listed on the special Value Cards below, you will receive a $2 savings on the regular price of a full service lubrication. It's easy. Just present your special Value Cards at the time of purchase.

You and your employees can use your cards over and over again as much as you like for the next six months.

All you have to do is have someone type or write in the name of your company on the cards, cut them out, and distribute them to your employees. Be sure to keep one for yourself, too! If you have more than 12 employees, just give us a call here at the office for additional cards. Do it today so your employees can get the full use of this valuable free benefit program.

(Optional: Signature and title of the chamber manager)

| minit-lube® | Compliments of (insert Cross-Promotion partner's name) |

VALUE CARD
The bearer of this card is affiliated with

and is entitled to a **$2 savings on the regular price of a full service lubrication** only at Minit-Lube. Cannot be combined with any other offer. Only one card per person per visit. Good only at the following Minit-Lube locations:
(insert address and phone, and locater)

No Appointment Necessary   Expires:

| minit-lube® | Compliments of (insert Cross-Promotion partner's name) |

VALUE CARD
The bearer of this card is affiliated with

and is entitled to a **$2 savings on the regular price of a full service lubrication** only at Minit-Lube. Cannot be combined with any other offer. Only one card per person per visit. Good only at the following Minit-Lube locations:
(insert address and phone, and locater)

No Appointment Necessary   Expires:

| minit-lube® | Compliments of (insert Cross-Promotion partner's name) |

VALUE CARD
The bearer of this card is affiliated with

and is entitled to a **$2 savings on the regular price of a full service lubrication** only at Minit-Lube. Cannot be combined with any other offer. Only one card per person per visit. Good only at the following Minit-Lube locations:
(insert address and phone, and locater)

No Appointment Necessary   Expires:

| minit-lube® | Compliments of (insert Cross-Promotion partner's name) |

VALUE CARD
The bearer of this card is affiliated with

and is entitled to a **$2 savings on the regular price of a full service lubrication** only at Minit-Lube. Cannot be combined with any other offer. Only one card per person per visit. Good only at the following Minit-Lube locations:
(insert address and phone, and locater)

No Appointment Necessary   Expires:

| minit-lube® | Compliments of (insert Cross-Promotion partner's name) |

VALUE CARD
The bearer of this card is affiliated with

and is entitled to a **$2 savings on the regular price of a full service lubrication** only at Minit-Lube. Cannot be combined with any other offer. Only one card per person per visit. Good only at the following Minit-Lube locations:
(insert address and phone, and locater)

No Appointment Necessary   Expires:

| minit-lube® | Compliments of (insert Cross-Promotion partner's name) |

VALUE CARD
The bearer of this card is affiliated with

and is entitled to a **$2 savings on the regular price of a full service lubrication** only at Minit-Lube. Cannot be combined with any other offer. Only one card per person per visit. Good only at the following Minit-Lube locations:
(insert address and phone, and locater)

No Appointment Necessary   Expires:

| minit-lube® | Compliments of (insert Cross-Promotion partner's name) |

VALUE CARD
The bearer of this card is affiliated with

and is entitled to a **$2 savings on the regular price of a full service lubrication** only at Minit-Lube. Cannot be combined with any other offer. Only one card per person per visit. Good only at the following Minit-Lube locations:
(insert address and phone, and locater)

No Appointment Necessary   Expires:

| minit-lube® | Compliments of (insert Cross-Promotion partner's name) |

VALUE CARD
The bearer of this card is affiliated with

and is entitled to a **$2 savings on the regular price of a full service lubrication** only at Minit-Lube. Cannot be combined with any other offer. Only one card per person per visit. Good only at the following Minit-Lube locations:
(insert address and phone, and locater)

No Appointment Necessary   Expires:

| minit-lube® | Compliments of (insert Cross-Promotion partner's name) |

VALUE CARD
The bearer of this card is affiliated with

and is entitled to a **$2 savings on the regular price of a full service lubrication** only at Minit-Lube. Cannot be combined with any other offer. Only one card per person per visit. Good only at the following Minit-Lube locations:
(insert address and phone, and locater)

No Appointment Necessary   Expires:

| minit-lube® | Compliments of (insert Cross-Promotion partner's name) |

VALUE CARD
The bearer of this card is affiliated with

and is entitled to a **$2 savings on the regular price of a full service lubrication** only at Minit-Lube. Cannot be combined with any other offer. Only one card per person per visit. Good only at the following Minit-Lube locations:
(insert address and phone, and locater)

No Appointment Necessary   Expires:

| minit-lube® | Compliments of (insert Cross-Promotion partner's name) |

VALUE CARD
The bearer of this card is affiliated with

and is entitled to a **$2 savings on the regular price of a full service lubrication** only at Minit-Lube. Cannot be combined with any other offer. Only one card per person per visit. Good only at the following Minit-Lube locations:
(insert address and phone, and locater)

No Appointment Necessary   Expires:

| minit-lube® | Compliments of (insert Cross-Promotion partner's name) |

VALUE CARD
The bearer of this card is affiliated with

and is entitled to a **$2 savings on the regular price of a full service lubrication** only at Minit-Lube. Cannot be combined with any other offer. Only one card per person per visit. Good only at the following Minit-Lube locations:
(insert address and phone, and locater)

No Appointment Necessary   Expires:

Figure 2-10   12-in-1 pieces receive 12 times the distribution of a standard value card.

type or write in the name of your business on the cards and distribute them to your employees. If you have more than 12 employees, call us here at the Chamber for additional cards. Do it today so your employees can get the full benefits of this exciting three-month program!

This 8½ × 11 sheet of card stock with the 12 cards went out to over 1000 Chamber members in this small city. A regular value card could have been used for this promotion, and there would have been 1000 cards distributed free. But, with this little twist, 1000 sheets were mailed out by the Chamber at no cost to the advertiser. Instead of 1000 cards getting out, the 1000 sheets were then cut up into 12,000 cards. It made a significant impact on sales.

Obviously, this particular version of the value card has limited application, and some have found it a little confusing. This program is a two-stage distribution. The person who receives the full sheet of 12 cards must have 12 people to hand the cards out to (11 plus him or herself). So it would not make sense to do 12-in-1 at a local factory. Each person who gets the piece is the only one using it. On the other hand, a local bank has many business customers. Each of the business customers has many employees, so by networking with your local bank, they can send out the 12-in-1 sheets to their business customers. In turn, the owner or manager of the business receiving the sheets from the bank cuts out the 12 cards, keeps one, and gives the other 11 away to employees. You get 12 for the price of 1.

You may find that you only do a 12-in-1 three or four times a year, but when you do them, you can get such a tremendous number of cards distributed that it is certainly worth learning how to do it.

The original version of the 12-in-1 was a direct mail piece. It worked great, but this newer version allows you to get the same thing without paying for the postage. In addition, and more importantly, this version allows you to transfer the responsibility of the discount to your cross-promotion partner.

TICKET-TO-EVENT

In your community, there are several special events such as con-
certs, trade shows, sporting events, and so on. Each of these
events is an opportunity for you to get free exposure and distribution of your advertising to a large number of people in a short
period of time.

The ticket-to-event is similar to a standard merchant certificate cross promotion with one enhancement: It is used as an
extra incentive by the show's promoter to help sell more tickets.
It is to the show promoter's advantage to mention this added
value in all of the advertising for the event.

Not only do you get free distribution of your piece, but you
get a mini-commercial inside a commercial. You get thousands
and possibly tens of thousands of dollars of media advertising,
all free to you. (See Figure 2-11.)

Trade show events are the easiest to use. These include auto
shows, home and garden shows, boat shows, gun shows, flea
markets, swap meets, bridal shows, antique car shows, county or
even state fairs, as well as a host of others.

Figure 2-11   Ticket-to-event cross promotion.

The ticket-to-event works particularly well when the promoter charges the audience a small cover charge. With your cross promotion, they can then advertise, "Admission is $2 at the door, but you'll get a certificate good for a $2 savings on your next purchase at [your store]." It gives the illusion that the admission is basically free since they are getting their money back in the form of a savings at your store.

To make it even more attractive for your promoter to work with you, you can provide "door busters" for the show. These are usually certificates good for free products or services, and are given to the first 25, 50, or 100 people to show up at the door. If you own a restaurant, or service-oriented business, then in addition to your standard cross-promotion certificate, you can provide, for example, 25 free services or products (i.e., free small pizza, free haircut, free oil change, free photo finishing). These will cost you a minimal amount, but the show promoter will hit this hard in the newspaper, radio, TV, and billboard advertising because it will get people there early.

The promoter's biggest responsibility is to get warm bodies at these shows so that the exhibitors, who have paid a premium to be there, will feel that they're getting their money's worth and will sign up again for next year's show. You help them do it, and you'll get free advertising.

◇ More Cross-Promotion Exercises

You're not finished yet! Do the following exercises for setting up the various types of cross promotions in your neighborhood. Use 10 examples in each category, then be sure to go back through your list and mark the ones who are already your customers:

1. 10 businesses that serve other businesses for 12-in-1s
2. 10 events (shows) for ticket-to-event promotions

Now you have a total of 45 opportunities listed for all of the exercises in this chapter. Out of those 45, you've identified the key people in those businesses who are already your customers. From that list, pick three who you think would be open to a cross promotion. Mark them with stars.

MORE FUN TO COME

In later chapters, you'll learn how to further infiltrate your community by working with charity and nonprofit groups, your own employees, and your customers. You will also learn to free media exposure from the news and advertising media.

Before you can approach the three key people you've just marked with stars, you have to know how to approach them and what to say. In the next chapter, you'll learn some easy ways to present your promotion so your cross-promotion partners will not turn you down.

Rejection-Free Skills for Community Cooperation

3

Before I struck out on my own, I was working for a small advertising agency. We had just landed our biggest account ever—one of the local banks. The CEO invited our entire staff over to the bank to get acquainted. He opened the informal meeting by telling us this story: He and a friend of his, the CEO of a large print shop, had played golf together every week for the past 10 years. One day while they were heading into the clubhouse, his friend asked him, "Dick, we've been playing golf together for 10 years now. How come your bank never uses my print shop?"

"My response was," he said very seriously as he looked very deliberately at each one of us, "you never asked me."

He went on to explain that he wasn't interested in winning advertising awards, nor was he concerned about impressing the CEOs of other banks. "I'm only interested in advertising that sells."

Until a sale is made, nothing happens. The same holds true for cross promotions and for all forms of streetsmart marketing. You have to sell your ideas and get people to act.

In this chapter, you'll learn the basics of how to set up these promotions. The ideas and techniques of this chapter are based on some very simple sales training, and they can also be used in other aspects of your business as well as in your nonbusiness activities.

Don't allow the term sales to scare you. Sales is nothing more than presenting your side of the story in such a way that the person you're presenting it to agrees with you and takes your suggested course of action. Almost everything we do in our lives involves some type of sales.

When you convince your child to get her homework done instead of going outside to play with her friends, that is a form of sales. When you convince your spouse to attend a certain dinner party because you know you'll meet some important people, that is sales.

Streetsmart sales techniques are not designed to trick someone into doing something they do not want to do. They are designed to help someone understand the true value and benefits of what you have to offer. There are no arguments, no tricks, no arm twisting, and no losers.

With streetsmart sales, you create an everyone-wins situation.

So far, you've learned the overall attitude of the streetfighter and several variations of the cross promotion. Now you will learn what to say and how to say it in order to convince someone in your community to distribute your advertising for free. It may sound impossible, and if you approached a merchant or major employer and asked him if he would pass out your advertising for free, it would be impossible. But as a streetfighter, your streetsmart marketing training prepares you to negotiate an alliance with all of your potential community cross-promotion partners.

There are 10 basic steps in setting up a cross promotion. By following these steps, you will be able to obtain the cooperation of many people in your area.

10 Steps for Setting Up the One-Way Cross Promotion

STEP 1 INTRODUCE YOURSELF

This is done in a low-key manner. Do not make your approach like a slick used-car salesperson, but rather as just another member of the community who came upon an idea that will benefit both of you. To establish rapport, be sure that you're not intimidating.

STEP 2 SHOW A SAMPLE OF YOUR CROSS PROMOTION

It is important to use actual samples rather than machine copies or a rough draft scratched on a yellow legal pad. That someone else has already done it seems to lend a stamp of approval. Since you're suggesting that you both adapt the concept specifically between the two of you, you can even use a sample from a totally nonrelated business.

If you don't have a real sample, you must do your first cross promotion with a good friend or customer. Use someone you've identified in your exercises from Chapter 2.

STEP 3 PRESENT THE "YOU" BENEFITS

Show it as an "added value" for his/her customers when they've paid their bill. It is an opportunity for him/her to show their customers appreciation for their business. You'll be learning about this in greater detail later in this chapter.

STEP 4 AGREE ON A DATE OF DISTRIBUTION

Distribution should usually be for a period on one week, or two at the most. After two weeks, most cross-promotion partners get tired and lazy, and the program becomes greatly weakened. Also, be sure to give yourself plenty of time to set it up. If you're not used to putting these promotions together, plan at least three weeks for your first few. After you get the hang of it, you'll eventually be able to set everything up in a week or so.

Once you agree on the time period of your distribution, you can decide on the expiration date. For most retail-type businesses, 30 days is fine. However, if your business is one in which the frequency of your customers' visits is less than weekly or even monthly, you might want to extend it.

For example, the expiration date on a restaurant promotion can be 30 days because a restaurant can be visited a couple of times a week. A hair salon is usually visited about once a month, an oil change once every four or five months, and a carpet store once every three to seven years. An expiration date longer than 90 days seems to be worthless.

The expiration must be kept reasonably tight in order to create a sense of urgency. The idea is to get the recipient of your certificate to act soon. The longer they have, the better the chance of them losing it or forgetting about you altogether.

STEP 5 GET THE WEEKLY CUSTOMER TRAFFIC COUNT

This is so that you will know how many special certificates to print. The reason this is done on a weekly basis is because, for many types of retail businesses, the customer frequency is on a weekly basis (as mentioned in Step 4). Remember, the purpose of a cross promotion is to get someone to try you for the first time. You wouldn't want to have a promotion with a grocery store for three months because most people go to the store about once a week. That would mean that those customers would receive 12 or 13 of your certificates. You would then lose impact and price credibility. Thus, you may not want to participate in a grocery store promotion in which your coupon is placed on the back of the cash register tapes. Usually the cost is reasonable, and since the grocery store is distributing them, you are transferring the responsibility of the discount. However, the grocery store usually wants you to be in the program for three months.

By the time the customer gets several of your coupons, it is no longer a special deal. They know they can get them anytime, and then your price credibility is lost. You will also lose money from discounting those people who would have paid full price.

To avoid this, use this motto: One at a time/one week at a time. This means that your overall goal is to set up at least one local promotion each week, and the distribution of that promotion should be only for a one-week period. The exceptions are those cross-promotion partners who have longer-term customer frequencies, such as hair salons, auto service centers, paint stores, shoe stores, and so on. Even then you do not want distribution to be more than a few weeks unless you can insure that the distribution is handled properly for the duration of the promotion.

STEP 6 GET THEIR LOGO

Placing the company logo of your cross-promotion partner on the promotion piece helps to transfer the responsibility of the discount. In addition, your partner will feel as if it's his/her promotion as well as yours. Using their logo will help you to gain their support of the promotion. The more you can do to show them the value they will receive, the better the response. Sometimes they can't use a logo without permission. If this is the case, just use the company name. But in most cases, this will not be a problem.

Another way to sell your promotion is to put the name of the owner or manager right under the logo (Figure 3-1). This gives the promotion a personal touch, but be sure to spell his or her name correctly.

Another idea is to use the signature of the owner or manager rather than just his or her printed name. This really makes it look official, and it also adds a nice touch. To do this, just have

Figure 3-1 McDonald's certificate passed out by the owner of their local Shell Gas Station.

the person sign his or her name with black ink on white paper in several sizes. Do not use blue ink because it won't reproduce properly when printed.

To add even more ego boosting, add a photo along with the signature. This can be used as a closing technique when your potential partner is almost hooked on your idea.

STEP 7 GIVE A FREEBIE

Use a gift certificate or free card, depending on the type of business. It could be worth between $5 and $10 in products or services from your store, with your cost being between $2 and $4. Examples of free items include a small pizza, an oil change, a hair cut, and a sandwich.

If your product or service is a high-ticket item, it becomes more difficult to give away a free item. With the apartment complexes we worked with, it was impossible to give away a free apartment. Instead, we used some contest prizes they had in stock from a contest they did the year before. There were T-shirts, coffee mugs, and visors. You may wish to use this idea. Just pick up some inexpensive items to give away in your promotion.

Warning: This is not a bribe! You are not telling them that if they do this promotion, they get a free gift. You must sell the promotion to each person on its own merits. The freebie is part of what I like to call the "glue": a kind of professional courtesy that bonds your partner to the promotion and insures that you'll get proper distribution.

STEP 8 FIND OUT HOW MANY EMPLOYEES ARE IN THE ORGANIZATION

Then explain that you realize bag stuffing, envelope stuffing, invoice stapling, and personally handing out your promotional material with the change requires extra effort from the employees, and that when you come back with their special thank you certificates, you will also provide special employee value cards for all the employees.

The value of the employee card needs to be of greater value than the cross-promotion certificate, but of lesser or equal value to the freebie given to the manager. For example, if your cross-promotion certificate is good for "25 percent savings" and you gave a "free card" to the owner, your employee card might be "buy one get one free."

Always keep in mind that the employees at your cross-promotion partner's business are usually the ones who will hand out these certificates. They can just as easily toss them in the trash, so you must do all that is necessary to gain their support. Providing these employees with their own benefit will show them why they should distribute your certificates.

One of the more interesting approaches for getting employee support was done at a franchise submarine sandwich restaurant. To get the employees of a department store behind the program, the restaurant owner brought over a few six-foot party subs and provided a free lunch. As the employees were enjoying their meal, she explained to them the details of what she called "this exciting program for your customers." A similar approach was used by a branch of a pizza chain when promoting with a gas station.

STEP 9 GO TO YOUR LOCAL QUICK PRINTER

Be sure to print extra copies for setting up future cross promotions.

STEP 10 KEEP YOUR KEY PLAYERS INFORMED

This includes your employees, your supervisors, other affiliated stores in your area, and the appropriate people at your local, regional, or national headquarters.

Display samples of the pieces so that your employees are aware of your promotion. There's nothing worse than having an excited customer come in your front door, proudly hand one of your employees a special certificate, and then be told, "I don't know if we can accept that. I'll have to check." That would definitely ruin the effect!

If your business has other stores that might be getting some of these certificates, be sure to inform them, too. It's a good idea to form an informal association of all your stores to share ideas. If you have a promotion that works particularly well, let them know, and they'll return the favor. By the same token, if you have a promotion that turned out to be a total bomb, save them from making the same mistake. The more people involved, the faster you will learn exactly what works and what doesn't.

WHAT TO SAY AND HOW TO SAY IT

The following is a transcript that you might follow when setting up a typical cross promotion. This should only be used as a guideline; you should put these basic concepts into your own words so it sounds natural and relaxed. Learn your presentation well. Never walk into a store with this book in your hand and read this script verbatim. Keep in mind that the entire process, once you are speaking with the decision maker, should take you under two minutes to complete.

YOUR INTRODUCTION

"Hi! I'm Jeff Slutsky, the owner of Jeff's Bar and Grill on Whittier Street just down the block. I've got something here that I thought was pretty interesting and thought you might like to see it."

[Hand him/her your cross-promotion sample.]

"Here's how it works. I would like to offer you the opportunity of providing your customers a way they can get more for their money, an added value, and kind of a special way you can say 'Thank you!' to your customers for shopping at your store. What do you think?"

[At this point, you wait for the question about the cost, which will be asked about 99 percent of the time. When you are asked how much it costs, you respond with . . .]

"Well, let me ask you a question. If it were free, would you do it?"

[They usually respond with something like "Free? Well, sure, why not?"]

As you shake hands, you say, "Fair enough." At this point you have approval, but you're not finished yet. You need to take care of some details.

Get the weekly customer count (if it's the type of business whose regular customers come in weekly). Ask, "How many customers do you run through here in a week?"

"Oh, about 1000."

"Great. By the way, have you been down to my place lately?"

"No, I haven't."

"Well, I'll tell you what. I would like you to be my guest when you get a chance. Here is a special card good for a free dinner." [Sign the card, date it, and hand it to him/her.]

"I need a good copy of your logo, preferably black on white, if you have it."

"How about using the one on our letterhead?"

"Perfect. Oh, how would you like your name to appear on the special thank-you certificate?"

"Ah, that's John Smith, Owner."

"Great. Would you like your signature on there, too? Your customers might really like that."

"Sure, why not."

If he/she wants a signature, get it in a couple of different sizes using a *black* pen on white paper. Next, set up the time.

"Let's see. Today is the 10th, so how about if I get your 1000 special thank you certificates to you by the 25th, and you hand one to each of your customers from the 26th through the 31st?"

"No problem."

"By the way, how many employees do you have?"

"There are about 27 in all."

"Well, I realize that it will take a little effort for them to personally hand these special certificates to each of your customers, and, obviously, we just can't have a stack of these sitting on the counter. So, when I return with your 1000 special thank you certificates, I'll also bring 27 2-for-1s for your employees. Okay?"

"Great! Thanks!"

"It was really nice meeting you, and I'll see you on the 25th."

THE REASON IT WORKS

First of all, as explained earlier, you're presenting the "you" benefits. Notice how many times the word "you" or "your" is used. Seven times! Everyone wants to know what's in it for them. They could care less about handing out your advertising for you. But by showing them what they get out of the arrangement, you get their cooperation.

One reason why this or any type of presentation works is because a question was asked. Question asking is so important that books are written on the subject. (See the Resource Guide.)

StreetSmart Sales Rule:

The person who asks the questions controls the conversation.

Bill Bishop says that "the person who asks the questions is in control of the conversation." In order to get your point across, you have to be in control. If the other person is asking you questions, you will spend all of your time answering them. Being on the defensive will keep you off course.

People think at about 1000 to 1200 words a minute, but they talk at only about 300 words a minute. The significance of this is that while you're telling your story, your prospect can think about seven times faster than you can talk, which gives him or her time to come up with objections and reasons not to believe you.

But if you're the one asking the questions, these decision makers have to pay attention. They cannot let their minds wander because they're required to respond to you. You're in control. You now have the advantage of thinking seven times faster than they talk, which gives you time to think of the most appropriate and convincing way to present your case.

There is another important aspect about asking questions. You can learn a great deal about the needs of the person you're talking to. People don't buy products or services (or even cross promotions); they buy solutions to problems. You don't buy a car; you buy a solution to your transportation problem. You don't buy a house; you buy a solution to your housing problem.

If you can help people to understand what their problems are, then you can offer your solutions. Closing the sale will then be the easiest part.

EMOTIONS VS. LOGIC

Another principle to remember is that people make decisions based on emotions backed by logic. You can give someone all the logical reasons to buy from you, but their final decisions will be made on the basis of their emotions.

Look back at the script. Notice how you present your case from an emotional point of view. You imply how much their customers will appreciate receiving something extra.

The type of question you ask is also important. In the

sample script, we ask the question, "What do you think?" We specifically do not want to ask, "Do you want to do it?" because this is a question that requires a yes or no answer. This type of question requires a decision. You don't want to do that because decision making is painful. Everytime you ask people to make up their minds about something, they appear to be in great pain. University studies have been conducted to prove this. Subjects were hooked to an elaborate computer monitor that recorded their reaction to certain stimuli. One test was to stick the subject in the arm with a sharp hatpin. Abnormal brain waves registered on the printout. Another test was to put the subject in a position where a decision had to be made, and the brain waves registered were almost exactly the same as when the subject was stuck by a pin. The conclusion is that decision making is painful, but interestingly enough, once the decision was made, whether it was right or wrong, the pain went away.

When approaching someone about a cross promotion (or any kind of decision-making situation), present your information in a way that will help them to avoid that pain.

To do this, do not ask decision-making questions. Do not ask questions that require a "yes" or a "no" answer, because those are painful. When you ask those kinds of questions and the person starts feeling the pain, he or she will do anything to get the pain to stop. Usually the solution will be to postpone making the decision. "Yes" or "no" answers are equally painful. To stop the pain, such responses as, "Let me think about it," or "I'll have to talk it over with my spouse" will be used.

These responses are only excuses to postpone making the decision and thus to avoid the pain.

You can help a person to avoid the pain by asking a question that does not require a decision. Instead, ask an opinion question. These are questions that start with what, why, who, when, or how. When you ask your cross-promotion partner the question, "What do you think?" you are asking that person for an opinion, not a decision. Everyone loves to give an opinion. Another term used for "opinion" questions are "open-ended" questions. Decision questions are referred to as "close-ended" questions.

No matter how good something sounds, people have a tendency to be skeptical. They know there's no free lunch, so they're looking for the catch. The obvious detail that comes to their minds is the cost. You purposely don't mention that it is free so that they will ask you about it. Since it's their natural tendency to object, you leave open the one objection with the strongest response.

Usually the response will be, "Well, it sounds pretty good, but how much does it cost?"

With their response they have regained control of the conversation. In my last book, *Streetfighting*, we were using the comeback, "It's free."

That would work about 25 percent of the time, which is a good approval ratio. Then, instead of using a statement, we began giving the same information in the form of a question. This raised the approval rate to over 50 percent. By responding with the statement, "It's free," you're inviting the response, "Well, let me think about it."

To delay in getting approval is to waste your valuable time. Furthermore, you will seriously jeopardize your chances of getting the promotion. Instead, respond with this question in order to regain control: "Let me ask you this: if it were free, would you do it?" (Make your voice go up when you say, "would you do it," as if you're just thinking of this off the top of your head.)

Now you've asked a "what . . . if" question. It's a hypothetical situation that again asks for an opinion, not a decision. There's no pain, so the response is usually something like, "Free . . . I guess, sure, why not, what the heck."

At that point, shake hands and say, "Fair enough." The promotion is on, and the decision was painless.

BUT I HAVE TO TALK IT OVER WITH MY SPOUSE

Dealing with objections is a very advanced sales training area, but there are simple techniques to overcome the one objection that you will most often get: "I have to talk it over with . . . (my husband, my wife, my supervisor, my boss, the owner, our legal department, my brother, my dog, etc.)."

Probably 99 percent of the time, they really don't have to talk it over with anyone. It is just an excuse to postpone making a decision. To deal with objections, follow these four steps:

1. Soften the Objection

2. Isolate the Objection

3. Get a Positive Opinion

4. Suggest Your Solution

Use this script to deal with this objection:

They have asked you how much it costs, and you have responded with, "If it were free, would you do it?" They might then say something like, "Sure, but I have to talk to my boss first."

At that point, you first respond with, "I understand," then you ask two questions: "Let me ask you this: other than talking it over with your boss, is there any other reason why you wouldn't be able to give me the 'go-ahead' right now?"

[Usually there isn't.]

"Then, in your opinion, is there any reason why you think your boss wouldn't want to do it?"

"No, but I really need to get her permission before I can do anything like this."

"Great. Let me make a suggestion. Why don't we get the ball rolling now, and in the meantime, you talk it over with your boss. If there's any problem, give me a call. Fair enough?"

This will help about half of the time. Once the manager has made the commitment, they usually don't even need permission. If they do, they're really going to sell it for you because they already made the commitment. Once they agree, continue on as you would normally do by finding out the customer count.

If you don't get an agreement, find out when the manager will have a decision, then return at that time. You might want to get a copy of the logo so you can follow up by phone. That way you can save yourself a trip. Also, forget the signature in this instance. Use the name and title only.

THE RATIONALE OF HANDLING OBJECTIONS THIS WAY

Soften the Objection—The immediate response is "I understand." No matter what somebody says to you when they object, you respond with "I understand." Do not try to argue with them, and do not use logic on them. They will not respond to logic. They will respond to emotion.

By saying "I understand," you're showing empathy. You have told them that you are looking at the problem from their point of view. This helps them to feel more comfortable and perhaps to drop their guard just a little. This is called a "softener."

Isolate the Objection—Next, stay in control and begin to dissipate their pain by asking the first of the two questions: "Let me ask ask you this: other than wanting to talk it over with your boss, is there any other reason we couldn't get the ball rolling now?"

This is called "isolating the objection." When people start to feel pain, they want to have a number of pain killers handy. Once you effectively answer their first objection, they'll come back with another excuse. Once you solve that one, they will have a third excuse. They always have one more excuse than you have answers. So, to avoid this game, we isolate. Once they answer this question with "no," and they usually do, they have told you that this is the only thing holding up the program.

It would be very difficult for them to come back with a second excuse. Some may try, but most won't. They subconsciously feel that they have the perfect pain killer, so they usually answer "no."

Get a Positive Opinion—The next question: "Well, in your opinion, is there any reason why you think your boss wouldn't want to do it?" (Your voice needs to go up high when you get to the "wouldn't want to do it" part. If it cracks a little, all the better.)

"Oh, it sounds like a great idea, I'm sure she'll like it, but I do have to run it by her since she's in charge of all this stuff."

Suggest a Solution—All the elements are now in place. Before you can offer a suggestion, you have to get all of the potential problems worked out before they are real problems. You know that running it by the boss is the only problem, and in the opinion of your partner, there is really no reason why it shouldn't be approved. Now you're ready to make your suggestion. Notice that you use nonthreatening terms such as "get the ball rolling."

Once they agree to "get the ball rolling," their pain goes away. Most of the time they won't even call the boss because there's no cost involved. Or if they do, they treat it much differently. Without this exercise, they might call the boss and say, "Hey, this guy came into the store and wants me to pass his advertising out for him. You don't really want to mess with it, do you?" They do this because there was no commitment.

But after you go through the little dialogue we just did, they approach the boss a little differently. "I just got us a great deal. This guy came into the store and wants to give us special certificates that we can hand out to our customers to give them more for their money. And guess what—I talked him into doing it for free. Pretty neat, huh?"

The chances of a supervisor killing the second approach is very slim.

Let's say you get the manager to "get the ball rolling," but she calls back a week later and says the boss shot it down. You are sitting in your office staring at 10,000 certificates with their logo on it that may as well be wastepaper.

Big deal! Okay, so you blew $100 once, but it doesn't happen often. You have to think of all the times you saved money by getting the other ten promotions approved using the technique. Even so, let's try to salvage it. As soon as they call to tell you it got shot down, you respond as if you're going into shock. "You gotta be kidding! I'm sitting here looking at 10,000 certificates with your logo and your name on it. Boy, is my boss going to be mad.

"I'm really sorry, but he just didn't want to do it."

"I am dead meat. What am I going to do? . . . I don't suppose there's any way you could just get out some of them for a few days—I'm really in a bind, and I'll be forever in your debt."

"I guess, I'll see what I can do. Go ahead and bring 'em out here."

It may be a little theatrical, but it does work. After all, your business is a stage; your customers and employees are the players, and you are the producer.

How You Say It Makes the Difference

The words you use and the way you say them makes all the difference in how a potential buyer or cross-promotion partner accepts your ideas. The phrasing of your questions makes all the difference in the response you get. People give appropriate responses to the questions asked, which is best illustrated in the following fable:

> A monk who just joined the monastery asked the Abbot for permission to smoke his pipe when he prayed. The Abbot responded by telling the new brother that he felt it was inappropriate and would have to refuse him his request.
>
> The brother went out to the courtyard only to see an old monk walking on the other side smoking a pipe. He quickly approached the older monk and told him that he was

confused. "I asked for permission to smoke my pipe when I prayed, and was not granted permission. Yet, I see that somehow you got permission to smoke your pipe. I'm confused, brother. Please tell me how you did it."

The older monk smiled slowly as he pulled his pipe out of his mouth and blew out some smoke. "Well, my brother," he said very slowly. "I asked the Abbot an entirely different question. I asked him if it was permissible to pray when I smoked my pipe. He told me that anytime was a good time for prayer."

TURN DOWNS

You want to get the most results out of each effort. Just as you now have a script for dealing with those managers who will not make a commitment until they talk it over with their boss, there is also a way to turn around a turn down.

If a potential cross-promotion partner decides not to use your cross promotion, thank them as you have been doing, and then hand that person a low liability VIP card (like the value card). Tell them that when they're in the market for your product or service, you would like to be considered.

Although you may not have reached a few hundred or a few thousand potential customers, at least you can get one. Then, when that person does use it, you have one more chance to convert that person to a cross-promotion partner. As you know, it's always much easier to set up a cross promotion with someone who is already a customer.

FISH BOWL

One great way to learn of all the potential cross-promotion partners who are already your customers is to have a business card drawing. For a couple of weeks, patrons put their business cards in a fish bowl for a free drawing. It makes little difference what you use as a prize, as long as it's a strong enough incentive to get people to toss in their business cards.

Have your drawing, then go through those cards. You'll find the names, business addresses, phone numbers, and title of each person. Owners, managers, personnel directors, CEOs, and other influencial people can make decisions about networking with your company.

They're already your customers, and they already know your company. Approaching these people about a cross promotion will be easy.

Getting More Information

You have learned that by asking questions that keep you in control of the conversation, you can get your partner to agree with your idea. You also know that you must ask the right kind of questions; decision questions are painful and opinion questions are not. Also, opinion questions give you the opportunity to learn more about your partner so you will know the best way to sell them on the idea.

There is a technique that is simple and yet effective. It's called the "echo," and it is used during the "probing" stage of a sale. At this stage in your relationship with a client, it's your objective to find out all you can. You can only learn by listening, not by talking. So keep your client talking, and in doing so, you're learning everything you need know in order to solve the client's problems and thus get the sale.

The echo technique is to simply take the last few words of whatever the client tells you and repeat those words back in the form of a question. This prompts your client to volunteer more and more details. Not only do you find out all this valuable information, which is later used to close the sale, but your client feels that you really care. Besides, people just love to talk about themselves; let them do it in a controlled way, and the sale will be yours.

For example, a client might say something like, "We're looking for a way to increase our sales on the local level."

The response would then be, "local level?"

"Yes, you see, we're already doing as much as we can with our national budget, so we need something that will enhance what we're already doing."

"Already doing?"

"Sure. We're spending about 5 percent of sales now on our advertising, and we feel we should be getting a bigger return?"

"Bigger return?"

This technique even works on a personal, nonbusiness level as shown by the following vignette.

A former girlfriend had picked me up at the airport. Usually after a big trip I'm pretty "vegged-out" and just want to quietly stare off into space until I get home. This particular character trait of mine is not in the best interest of developing and maintaining a warm and caring relationship.

I decided right then and there that I would break myself out of that rut and show my affection and interest by asking about her day. She replied with great enthusiasm, "It was an absolutely crazy day. We had this corporate executive from the home office conduct a surprise evaluation."

Using the echo technique I responded, "evaluation?"

"Right. You see, every so often they send some corporate hot-shot down to make sure that we're doing everything we can, especially to see that our sales levels are on target."

"On target?"

"Yes. Our goal is to increase over last year by 12 percent and if we all do it, we get a special bonus."

"Bonus?"

"Oh, it's great! When we increase by 12 percent, they're

going to send everyone in our department on an all-expense-paid trip to St. Thomas."

"St. Thomas?" . . .

During the 30-minute ride home from the airport, using the echo technique, I probably didn't say more than 25 words, yet I knew everything about the past few days of her life.

How to
Profit from
the Nonprofits

The most exciting, rewarding, and profitable streetsmart marketing that you can generate are the community service programs that you can provide to your neighborhood non-profit organizations. Not only do these programs offer you the same benefits as cross promotions, but they also create high-impact exposure and tremendous goodwill throughout your community.

To achieve this level of "streetfighterhood," subscribe to the community service concept of "high visibility/low liability." This means that each community service program should create a great deal of exposure and goodwill, but more importantly, each should generate much new business. At the same time, the cost in both time and money should be very little. This is achieved by creating the perfect "everyone wins" situation.

When looking at any community service promotion, you must ask yourself whether you are advertising or whether you are giving money away. If you want to make a donation, that's wonderful—but don't confuse that with advertising.

If you want to buy an ad in the high school yearbook or your church bulletin, that's great—but don't confuse that with advertising.

If you can afford to make donations to worthy causes, you

should. It's important and proper that you do. Just don't expect a return on your investment.

Look at it this way. If a nonprofit group comes to you for a donation, you can afford to give them a little money. But if you provide them a means by which they could raise all the money they need for their project, you're actually providing a much better public service than making your small donation.

Hole-in-One

A good example of streetsmart community service is the quick print owner who was approached by the promoter of a pro/amateur celebrity golf tournament. This major week-long annual event is covered by live broadcast from all three network affiliates and the local independent TV station. All the radio stations do remote broadcasts from the country club, and the newspapers provide daily coverage. Big name celebrities and golf pros team up with local amateurs. The proceeds go to a worthy cause.

The quick print owner was asked to be a sponsor, which meant a donation of $750, a mention in the program, and his name, along with 19 others, on a little plaque. This was not much exposure for $750.

He responded by saying that this event was so worthwhile that he wanted to do something very special. He would put up a $10,000 cash prize for the first person to get a hole-in-one on the 9th hole. Of this, $5000 would go to the golfer and $5000 would be donated to the charity. His offer generated much excitement. It added a new dimension to the tournament. He personally was interviewed by every TV and radio station. He even got his photograph, along with a large reproduction of his company check with the logo, right on the front page of the newspaper. You couldn't buy that kind of exposure, and he easily got $10,000 worth.

But there was some risk. What if someone actually scored a hole-in-one on the 9th hole? Just in case, he took out an insurance policy from Lloyds of London to protect himself in case someone did get the big prize. The cost of the policy was only $450—$300 less than the sponsorship, yet he totally dominated the tournament.

I was having lunch with him at the country club the day the offer was announced. Three different people came up to him during lunch to congratulate him and thank him for his contribution to the program.

It was such a success that he has done the same program every year since. Guess what happened just three years later? Someone scored a hole-in-one on the 9th hole, and he got tens of thousands of dollars worth of free publicity once again.

Of course, his insurance premium in following years probably went up a little, but the money was well-spent for the amount of impact, goodwill, and exposure that he received.

DELUGE GUN

In my book *Streetfighting*, I used a fund-raising story in which a local volunteer fire department went from business to business trying to get donations so they could purchase a Deluge Gun—a very important piece of equipment that they needed.

They weren't having much success, but then they approached the manager of a pizza restaurant. He asked, "If I could provide you a way to raise all the money you needed for your Deluge Gun—would you be willing to work your tails off for a couple weeks?"

They said that they would, since they were already working their tails off and getting nowhere. The manager told them that in three weeks, on a Wednesday, he would donate half of all the evenings receipts to the cause. He also told them that his average

Wednesday was only about $500, so they would really have to work hard to get people into his restaurant so that they could raise the money they needed.

They did. They passed out fliers to people. They got free mentions on the local radio station and in the newspaper. They came out with their truck and their dalmatian and gave away more fliers in the parking lot of the restaurant the Saturday before. They put posters in almost every window in town—including another restaurant down the street! The only thing the manager did was to put up an announcement on his marquee sign and have a placemat made, that was used for one week (Figure 4-1).

Wednesday was a huge success. The place was packed. The volunteers and their spouses were even helping to wait on customers. They had a great time doing it, and they raised a tremendous amount of money. Now everyone in that city thinks that particular restaurant was personally responsible for raising the money for the life-saving equipment.

Goodwill and free exposure were obviously generated from this program, but with the streetsmart marketing approach, those are just the byproducts of a good community service program. The primary result for the restaurant was that they got many new customers in the front door and eating their food. This program got customers to buy and try. That's the critical difference between a streetfighter's approach to community service and the "warm and fuzzy" approach. Without trial, without getting customers into your location to give you a shot, you lose out. But with it, you can afford to do much more in your community.

SMALL IMPROVEMENT WITH OIL CHANGE

The program just described was classic. It had all of the elements needed for a successful community service program—

Let Yourself Go!

Pizza Hut.

This strange looking thing could save your life.

Coming to Pizza Hut® on July 25th could help buy it.

It's called a "Deluge Gun." It's a $1200 piece of fire fighting equipment that's badly needed by the New Haven Volunteer Fire Department.

The New Haven Pizza Hut restaurant wants to help them buy it, and here's how . . .

On Wednesday, July 25th, 50¢ out of every $1.00 spent with us at regular menu prices will go directly towards the purchase of the Deluge Gun!

So tell all your friends, bring your family and come on in for a good meal *and* a good cause!

Dine in or Carry Out

The New Haven Pizza Hut® restaurant in cooperation with The New Haven Volunteer Fire Department.

Figure 4-1 The only thing the manager did was to put up an announcement on his marquee sign and had a placemat made that was used for one week.

91

but even so, it can be improved upon. That's exactly what happened in a similar program done by a quick oil change center in Oregon.

The managers and their supervisors attended our full-day "Streetfighting" seminar, which is how we kick off a long-term customized development program for a client. The restaurant/volunteer fire department story was used as an example of a community service "biggie"—the type of promotion you do only once or twice a year.

The two improvements that were added to this community service program were (1) back out the break-even point and (2) use a bounce-back certificate, compliments of the charity group.

These two ideas were tested when the manager of the oil change center got a letter asking for a donation of goods or services for a charity auction to raise money for the Neurofibromotosis Foundation (Figure 4-2). Normally the manager would have tossed it out, but since he was now an official streetfighter, he gave us a call.

They were asking for a donation of merchandise instead of cash, which was a good sign. That always makes it easier to work with a group. So we made a conference call to find out the details of the program.

This disease, we found out, is a disfiguring genetic disease that affects 3000 children in the state of Oregon alone. The chairperson of the project had a five-year-old son who had the disease, and most of the volunteers were parents of children who had it.

At that point, we knew it was a very worthwhile cause. The only problem we saw was that the group was very small. Yet, they were very motivated. So we donated five free oil change gift certificates to the event, with a retail value of $100. She was very excited and almost in tears. Apparently, we were the first to respond to the mail request.

Then we suggested another fund raiser for their group. We offered to take a Wednesday (not our best day, but not our worst) and give them half of the day's receipts over the break even point.

Change Your Oil and Change a Life

 ®

**National
* Neurofibromatosis
Foundation**

You can help raise money for the research of NF, a disorder caused by gene mutation or inherited, that affects thousands of people here in Oregon.

When you change your oil at the Minit-Lube in Beaverton (Hwy. 217 & Beaverton-Hillsdale Hwy.) on Wednesday August 13th, half of all proceeds will go to the NF Foundation for research.

You Can Help

50% of your donation will be tax deductible

Wednesday August 13th

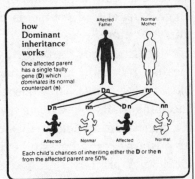

how **Dominant inheritance works**

One affected parent has a single faulty gene (**D**) which *dominates* its normal counterpart (**n**)

Each child's chances of inheriting either the **D** or the **n** from the affected parent is 50%

 ®

11150 S.W. Beaverton-Hillsdale Hwy. ● Beaverton, OR 97005 ● 626-3536

Figure 4-2 Donation of goods or services for a charity auction to raise money for the Neurofibromotosis Foundation.

We normally did about 20 cars on a given Wednesday at that time of year, so after the first 20 cars, they would get half of everything.

This little improvement over the restaurant promotion did a few things. First, it let us know just how motivated our volunteer group was. If they did absolutely nothing to help generate business, they still would have made about $200. But they knew that they really had to aggressively promote the event if they hoped to raise significant money for their cause. It removed all of our client's risk while it created a stronger motivation for success.

A business owner can afford to do this because it does not affect projected sales. It is not the intention to make money from this event. But at the same time, it shouldn't cost anything. The biggest benefit, of course, is the new customers who will come into your store.

This nonprofit group was aggressive. They appeared on a local TV talk show, made announcements on the radio, and had a blurb in the paper. They passed out fliers in parking lots of local shopping malls. Now if *you* try to do that, you get in trouble; but if a charity group does it, they can get away with it. They also put up posters everywhere and even got the printing donated by the local quick printer!

The day of the event, they decorated the store with balloons and handmade banners. They put homemade cookies in the lobby with a collection box for added donations. They even helped out by cleaning the windshields and vacuuming the cars while they were getting serviced.

That day there were a total of 43 cars—23 more than the auto service center normally did on a Wednesday. They raised over $300 for the cause, and they got free exposure, goodwill, and 23 new customers who had never used their service before.

There was one other little improvement. When you do a program such as one of these two, you allow many new customers to try you out at your store who have not been there before. Furthermore, these customers are trying you out under unique circumstances. You now have a perfect opportunity to invite them back one more time under more normal circumstances without fear of hurting your price credibility.

At another promotion, which was a grand-opening event, the service center handed out a bounce-back certificate (Figure 4-3). "Bounce backs" are given to your own customers, and for that reason, I shy away from them; they're already my customers. However, during a special event like the two mentioned, you want to provide an incentive to bring them back one more time because they're brand new customers. You can give the responsibility of the discount to the charity group. The certificate could say, "Compliments of the Neurofibromotosis Foundation."

Even in the grand-opening sample shown, the store manager takes responsibility for the promotion. Since in this particular situation every customer coming in is new, you would not have discounted them repeatedly. It's therefore safe to do this.

SOMETHING BORROWED

Sometimes you can tie into a good community service project without giving away anything, yet still get exposure, goodwill, and the chance for new customers. A stereo store loaned $10,000 worth of sound equipment to a group sponsoring a haunted house to raise money for a charity. Since the sound equipment was a major part of their haunted house, the stereo store received a cosponsorship along with the local radio station doing all the promoting.

As a result of their generosity, the stereo store got their logo on all of the fliers and posters, as well as a mention in the newspaper and radio ads. This was a great deal of exposure at no cost to them.

After the month-long fundraiser was over, the store had a perfect excuse to run a sale on $10,000 worth of slightly used stereo equipment from the haunted house.

One improvement they could have made was to provide each person going through the haunted house a special

Dear Minit-Lube Customer,

Thank you for coming to our Grand Opening Celebration. We hope you like our service and will give us the opportunity of serving you again in the near future. Save this special "Thank You" certificate for your next visit and you'll save $2.

Sincerely,

Steve E. Loski

Steve Loski
Manager

Good only at the following Minit-Lube® locations:

**521 N.E. 181st • 665-7303
On the Corner of 181st & Glisan
Across from Pay 'N Pak**

No Appointment Necessary

QUAKER STATE®

minit-lube

SAVE $2

This special "thank you" entitles you to a $2 savings on the regular price of your next full service lubrication visit. Only one special "thank you" per visit. Not valid in combination with any other offer.

Valid only at the following Minit-Lube locations:

**521 N.E. 181st
Portland, Oregon**

QUAKER STATE
MOTOR OIL

**We feature
Quaker State
products**

"Look for the Stripes™"

Expires
10/26/86

certificate with some offer to motivate them to visit the stereo store in the near future. Don't forget that bounce back. In their case, it could have been compliments of the local charity chapter and the cosponsoring radio station.

Allowing organizations to use your parking lot or building for their fundraiser is a good way to get a little extra exposure for yourself at no cost. Whether the fundraiser is a car wash or a cookie sale, don't forget the bounce-back certificate, because with it you'll get a number of potential new customers to visit you. The certificate is that little extra push to get them to try you out the first time.

A restaurant operator in the Los Angeles area allowed the local high school band to offer a gift-wrapping service during Christmas time. The kids set up a little display on the restaurant's land. With a $2 donation per box to the high school band, they would wrap a gift. The high school band promoted the service, which brought more people to the restaurant—at no cost. They raised over $2000, and just by letting them use a small area of his land, he became a hero. Now that's streetsmart community service.

When asked what he would do with the promotion to make it even more successful next year, the operator responded with, "Add a bounce-back certificate to put in the gifts that are being wrapped and to give to each of the gift givers."

It was interesting how this particular promotion came about. It started as a chain of community service events, the first of which was in a Buckboard Days parade. The restaurant operator had a convertible car in the parade with a chicken-character passenger called "Doodles." During the parade, they handed out 2000 free sandwich cards. Just ahead of them in the parade was the high school band. They became friends. Five hundred cards were redeemed. Not bad. Three hundred of them were stepped up to a full meal.

When the mall needed a band to welcome Santa, the restaurant operator contacted the high school band and offered each member a free sandwich for their musical talents. The band and the mall management loved it, and since the restaurant put the deal together, Doodles was right there with the band.

From one event came two others, and each time the store got more and better results.

GUIDELINES FOR COMMUNITY SERVICE "BIGGIE" PROMOTIONS

Have a Specific Item and Price—To increase your effectiveness, it's usually best to have a specific item and/or a specific price for the fundraiser. It makes a much greater impact in the mind of the consumer to tell them you're raising money for playground equipment or marching band uniforms than to tell them you're just raising money. Also, if you can say you need to raise $550, your neighbors can more clearly see what is needed and are more likely to respond to the cause. If you combine the two, as in "we need $550 for band uniforms," it makes it very clear to the public what the goals are.

Back a Local Cause—Make sure the cause you rally behind is a good local cause. You want to target a cause that hits close to home—your home in your community.

During the renovation of the Statue of Liberty, many merchants wanted to help with the fund raising. This would be fine for a store located in New York, but if you're anywhere else, it is better to do a fundraiser to renovate the "Statue of Irving," or whatever local cause there may be.

In Oklahoma City, there is a fine restaurant on top of a bank building. The manager put together a number of community involvement programs that tied directly in with the Oklahoma City community and with his clientele, who were upscale and affluent.

One promotion was a $100-a-plate dinner that raised money for a much-publicized heart transplant. A local person needed the operation, and a very aggressive committee headed by a very prominent businessman conducted the fundraisers. The manager merely provided the dinners at cost. He also conducted fundraisers for the local philharmonic.

With our clients around the country and even in other parts of the world, we've helped to raise money for all kinds of transplants and other life-saving things such as equipment and facilities. There have also been countless programs for equipment such as uniforms, athletic equipment, school supplies, and so on. In every case, the business also benefited directly from the promotion while helping to raise money for such worthy causes.

An interesting opportunity presented itself for a four-store formal wear franchisee. After attending a Streetfighting workshop at an annual convention, the owner developed a program for the prom season (his biggest season) to help bring awareness to the high school kids about the dangers of drinking and driving.

He approached the local CBS affiliate with his idea of giving a special "I Survived the Prom of '88—Don't Drink & Drive" t-shirt to each student who came into one of his stores and agreed to sign a document that committed them to not drinking and driving on prom night. To qualify, they also had to get measured for their tux at his store. This gave him the opportunity to rent them their formal wear for prom night.

At first he thought he would need to buy a few thousand t-shirts, but when the TV station said that with the impact they would create he would need 20,000, he had to give it a little thought. The TV station was going to create such an impact with this promotion that it could possibly provide him the opportunity to totally dominate the prom market. But, even at a cost of only $1.85 per t-shirt, he still had to lay out $37,000. Now his low-cost promotion was running into some real money.

Normally, when a promotion begins to cost too much, you walk away from it; but after really looking at the facts and figures, he took a different attitude.

First, his major competitor was aggressively promoting a $5 discount on tux rentals and spending well over $10,000 to support the discount promotion. He had to find a way to remain competitive. He would have had to spend a fortune on advertising media to offer a $5 discount as well. This is not a streetsmart solution, especially when it forces you to spend a fortune on mass media advertising and at the same time gives you a discount image in your community.

With the t-shirt promotion, cosponsored by the CBS TV station, he could charge full price for his rentals and give away the t-shirt as an added value. He would come out $3.15 ahead on every rental, plus he would get free advertising and impact in the community—enough to get rid of 20,000 t-shirts. He could not lose! After looking at it like that, it was much easier to justify the expense.

FUNERAL HOME

There was a funeral home in Florida that, at the end of the year, offered a free funeral to anyone who would come to one of their locations to sign a paper stating that they are stupid and plan to drink and drive on New Year's Eve; and if they die because of it, they get a free funeral. One person signed up.

But the funeral home got a lot of free press and was able to make a very valuable point to the community about the dangers of drinking and driving.

APPLAUSE VIDEO

The owner of a video rental store conducted one of the most beautiful community involvement programs ever.

When the movie *Platoon* came out on home video, he offered any Vietnam veteran the opportunity to rent it free of charge. If the veteran did not have a VCR, one would be provided free. If he was disabled and unable to come to the store, it would be delivered free.

This program had a great impact on the community. The program was mentioned on two different local TV news programs, on radio, and in the newspaper. The video rental store owner got free exposure, but more importantly, this program had tremendous impact because it was his way of giving some recognition to veterans. And they appreciated it. With this type of community service, you get some very loyal customers. This is something you can't buy with the more traditional forms of advertising. He did it by being StreetSmart and by genuinely wanting to do something special for his community.

THE BUCK STARTS HERE

In addition to your major fund-raising efforts and community promotions, you can also offer a very simple on-going program called "donation dollars." It can be used all year long by any worthy nonprofit organization.

It's very similar in concept to the basic merchant-certificate cross promotion mentioned in Chapter 2, with some slight variations. First of all, each piece is printed on both the front and back, usually six to a standard sheet of paper, so that they resemble a dollar bill (Figure 4-4).

Let's say that the local Boy Scouts are going door-to-door selling raffle tickets to raise money to buy playground equipment. The grand prize is a bike. A Boy Scout knocks on your door. He explains that he's selling raffle tickets. You ask how much they cost.

"Each ticket is $1.00, but with every one you buy, you

Figure 4-4 **Each piece is printed front and back so that they resemble dollar bills.**

Gold for: Optimist Club

Gold for you!

Your local McDonald's® supports a wide variety of community projects. Perhaps the Golden Arches™ can provide you a golden opportunity with your next community project. Contact your local McDonald's manager for further details. And remember, "It's A Good Time For The Great Taste!"® of McDonald's famous golden brown French Fries.

Not valid with any other offer. Limit one "McDonald's Gold" per person per purchase. Cash value 1/20th of one cent. Show your Gold at time of purchase.
Owner/operator: For reimbursement send to 279 South Sandusky St., Delaware, Ohio 43015.
Valid only at: 279 South Sandusky St.   Offer Expires: 4/31/86

COMPLIMENTS OF
SUMMIT CITY TRACK

Good only at these Pizza Hut® restaurants:

ALL FORT WAYNE LOCATIONS
NEW HAVEN • AUBURN • BLUFFTON • DECATUR
WARSAW • PLYMOUTH • KENDALLVILLE
VAN WERT • NORTH MANCHESTER • WABASH

$1.00 off the regular menu price of any Large Pizza Hut® pizza.

Offer Expires   August 31, 1981
One Coupon per Person per Visit
© 1980 The Advertising Company

• One Pizza Hut Buck •

SAVE 50¢   SUBWAY® Token   SAVE 50¢

A TOKEN FOR...   Noblesville High School   A TOKEN FOR YOU!

Offer good at participating Subway Restaurant listed below

Buy any footlong sandwich or regular salad and save 50¢!
Or buy any Snak size sandwich and save 25¢

Cannot be combined with any other discount or special.
Only one token per person.

Noblesville Plaza • 577 Westfield Road • 773-7057
Offer Expires January 31, 1986

get a dollar off your next purchase at Pizza Hut (or 50¢ off at Subway, or free fries at McDonald's, or $1 off your next oil change at minit-lube, etc.).

The charity group could be selling such things as candy, cookies, raffle tickets, and magazine subscriptions. It really doesn't matter. But when they ask for money, they get to throw in this little extra bonus for you. By adding value to the item for sale, the person selling for the charity feels that it's easier to sell. If they feel that it's easier to sell, they try harder and therefore sell more.

Now, what do you get? First of all, you're getting a live, five-second commercial, door-to-door in your neighborhood, by a high-visibility group such as the Boy Scouts, the Campfire Girls, the high school band, the March of Dimes, or B'nai Brith. Plus, you get your "donation-dollars" distributed free to all those that buy what they're selling. As a result, you seemingly contribute tens of thousands of dollars each year to charity—but they're product dollars, not real dollars, and only of value when a purchase is made.

You choose an offer that's right for you. It does not have to be worth a dollar. It also doesn't necessarily have to be a strong offer. This is very much like a cross promotion, but to maintains its integrity, only use this particular piece for community involvement.

The front side of the piece is generic. It explains what the program is about and that if you have a worthy cause you should call the local manager. In this way, the program somewhat builds itself with mirrors.

The back side contains the offer and the name of the charity group. With this piece, you only put the name of the group. You don't use their logo. The only two things that change are the name and the expiration. When a group wants some of your "bucks," you need only make a five-minute phone call to your quick printer and tell him/her the name of the group and the expiration date. A representative from the charity group picks them up at the printer when they're ready, so the time you spend on the promotion is small.

You can even have your printer preprint the front sides of your "bucks" in large quantities, and then do shorter runs of the customized reverse side. That will save you quite a bit of money in printing if you plan to use a lot of these. It's a good idea to use if for awhile before you do a large run.

A Token Gift

The manager of a submarine sandwich shop was approached by a high school for a six-foot submarine sandwich to be used as a door prize at their big annual fundraiser, which was an all night dance on New Year's Eve at the high school.

The manager went to the chairperson of the dance and asked her if it would help ticket sales if they could give everyone who bought a ticket a 50¢ rebate at no cost to them. The chairperson was good at math, and she immediately paid attention. Then the manager pulled out a "Subway Token" and explained that for every ticket they sold, they could also give each buyer one of these special certificates, which would make that ticket even more valuable. She loved the idea.

They sold 1000 tickets and consequently distributed 1000 tokens, of which 500 were redeemed! This is unheard of, and you certainly shouldn't expect that kind of redemption; but it did happen in this case, and it really helped to boost the sales of that store. The manager was trying to target the high school kids, and this gave him a great start.

This is an example in which donation is fine and may get you a little exposure, but by taking the promotion to its logical conclusion, you actually bring customers into your store to try you out. If you present it properly to the group, they'll thank you for your contribution.

GETTING YOUR DONATION DOLLARS OFF THE GROUND

To first let people know that you have such a valuable community service as your "donation dollar" program, use a flier (Figure 4-5). This particular flier serves a number of purposes. First, you get a list of all the nonprofit organizations in your community. This is usually available free or for a minimal charge from your local chamber. Mail the flier to everyone on the list.

The same piece can then be used to promote your "donation dollars" internally at your store. This is where you start to take your own customers and employees and turn them into streetfighters for you. Notice that the flier has a certificate at the bottom. This is used when mailing out the flier to nonprofit organizations to make them aware of your program. When distributing this same flier in your store, omit the certificate at the bottom or you'll discount your own customers. Just have your printer cut off the bottom section with the certificate on it. That's much less expensive than printing two different fliers.

In addition to printing fliers for internal distribution, take your original artwork while it's at your printer's and have it enlarged to 11 x 17 inches. It will be done on paper that feels more like a photograph and that is called a PMT, film positive, or velox. Then get some colored art board and paste it down. You will then have a very nice poster to hang in your store.

This type of program can be done as needed, but don't count it as one of your weekly cross promotions. It's a nice way of helping numerous worthy groups in your community without costing you a lot of money and time. It's also a great way to get people to

IF YOU'VE GOT A GOOD CAUSE...
MINIT-LUBE HAS $25,000 WORTH OF LOCAL HELP FOR:

(insert name of community, big and bold!)

Raising funds for your neighborhood or community projects may have become increasingly difficult in recent months. If so, all of us here at your local Minit-Lube would like to help you . . . and here's how:

It's called **"Minit-Money"**™ and as you can see from the sample, its good for a $1.00 savings on the regular price of a full service oil change and lubrication.

Whether your group is holding a Raffle, Dance, Candy Sale, Car Wash, Bazaar or other current event, giving a Minit-Money with every purchase seems to remarkably increase the dollars raised!

Help for you, too!

In addition to help for your organization, we would like to offer you a special reward for helping your community. We realize that fund raising and other valuable community programs and projects are time consuming and even a lot of extra miles on your car. So, as a way of showing our appreciation for your efforts, please feel free to use the special "Thank-You" certificate and we look forward to seeing you very soon at our Minit-Lube.

And as our way of making a contribution to our community, we've set aside $25,000 worth of Minit-Money for your fund raising projects in the coming year. To find out if your group qualifies, just contact us at the phone number listed below:

(insert store address, locator, phone and Manager's name)

Figure 4-5 If you have a valuable community service such as a donation-dollar program, you use a flier.

stop asking for donations. Convert them from asking for cash to asking for the "donation dollar." They'll love you for it.

As you'll recall, you are going to plan on doing at least one promotion a week as your streetsmart marketing goal. Donation dollars are the only type of promotions that don't count as your weekly promotional effort. All of the other "biggie" type promotions, and even some of the not-so-biggie promotions, can count. Donation dollars is something you do on an on-going basis. If ten different groups want them one week, you provide them all.

Turning a Promotion into Community Service

As a part of your streetsmart marketing, always be on the lookout for ways of converting a standard, everyday type of promotion into community service. It allows you to have your promotion and sell your products and services, but by using a community service project, you get more for your effort.

TRADE-IN SALES

Trade-in sales work when you can get a customer to bring in a used item that has some value to you or a nonprofit group. In return, you provide the customer with a discount on a new item.

Many times you could have just as easily offered the discount or savings without the trade-in item, but because you require a trade-in, you protect your price credibility and at the same time turn a standard sale into a community involvement program.

WARM IDEA

A woman's ready-to-wear chain in Indiana has a coat trade-in sale every Christmas. They allow their customers to bring in their old coats, as long as they are in decent shape, and they then get a discount on any new coat in stock. The old coats are then cleaned and donated to needy families.

FOCUSING ON THE NEEDY

A certain optician allowed his customers to bring in any pair of old glasses for a discount on any new glasses. The old ones were then donated to needy people.

PULPIT POWER

An investment company used a community service angle to increase their IRA sales. One of their key marketing strategies for selling their IRA programs was to advertise a free investment seminar. They would provide a one-hour program, which generated some great leads.

This was very successful, but it was made even more successful when one of their agents turned this program into a church fundraiser. Instead of advertising in the local newspaper at great expense, he approached a local church organization that wanted to raise money. He offered to pay them $2 per person for every qualified church member who came to his one-hour seminar, that would be held at the church.

If they got at least 50 or more, there would be a special bonus, and if there were 100 or more, the church would get an even bigger bonus.

This approach totally removes the risk from advertising. With the old way, he would pay for the advertising whether it worked or not. This community service approach is risk-free, since he only pays for each qualified person who shows up. In addition, giving the money to charity gives him a good-guy image in that neighborhood.

The church group would make phone calls, send out fliers, make announcements from the pulpit and at other meetings, and generally motivate their congregation to participate. The agent's only cost was when he got results.

COMMUNITY-SERVICE REVIEW

1. Streetsmart community involvement involves programs that get you free distribution of your advertising message. The goodwill and free exposure you get are "brownie points."

2. These programs should cost very little in time and money.

3. When committing to a major fundraiser, make sure that it requires people to try your product or service. The donation is performance-based, like a commission, and it only makes money when it is successful.

4. Look for good local causes. Tie into something in the neighborhood. Having a specific price and/or item helps.

5. Don't confuse advertising and donations. Ask yourself if you truly expect to receive a return on your investment. If you don't, that's fine if you want to make the donation, but don't call it advertising.

6. Look for one or two "biggie" type promotions for the year, but use your donation dollars and other types of community services throughout the year.

◇ Community Service Exercises

1. Write down 10 organizations that you can provide donation dollars to in your neighborhood. Out of the 10,

mark the ones where an influential representative of that organization is a customer of yours. You'll probably know who they are because they've tried to sell you some advertising or a raffle ticket in the last six months.

2. Write down 5 potential organizations for your annual "biggie" promotion. Also mark the ones where one of your customers is in that organization.

3. Write down at least 5 disasters, or emergency-type events, that happened in your community in the past 12 months. This could be anything from a tornado ripping apart a house, floods, accidents, disease, and so on. Then, for each one you can remember, figure out a strong community service tie-in that you could have done to both help them and help your business.

   Obviously you can't plan a disaster promotion, but when a disaster happens in your community, you have to act fast. This exercise helps you to understand just how you can help if the time should come when it is needed.

4. Write down all of the major sales or special programs you had in the past 12 months. Then write down how you could have turned those promotions into a community service program.

WE PRACTICE WHAT WE PREACH

While presenting our Streetfighting seminar for National Video at their annual convention in Freeport, Bahamas, I found out that later that evening they would be having an auction for the National Video Family Fund Foundation. Many suppliers donated items for the auction; included was the actual headband used by Sylvester Stallone in the making of *Rambo III*. As soon as I found out about the charity auction, I donated my sample Profit Package audio/video program. The announcement of my donation was made prior to my presentation, which brought applause from the organization. Of course, they explained the entire program in detail, along with its $400 value. As a result, I was a hero at their convention and we sold an additional 25 Profit Packages during the convention.

Surefire Strategies for Free Local Publicity

StreetSmart Marketing would be incomplete without a close look at how you can get free local publicity in your local news media. Before we discuss the "how-tos" of getting free publicity, it's very important to show you the power and value of this exposure.

THE POWER OF PUBLICITY

Remember that your customers have a tendency to tune out most advertising, so when you buy time on your local radio or TV station or space in the newspaper or on a billboard, you have to have a strong message and strong frequency to get them to remember your message. Later, you'll be learning how to get the most out of the advertising media. But at the same time, you can get exposure in the mass media, break through the advertising clutter, and make tremendous impact—and it won't cost you a penny! That's a power combination for any streetsmart marketeer.

While most people may be getting a beer or getting rid of a beer during the commercials, they do tune into the programs.

When you get publicity on a news show or a local talk show, you then become the very reason they watch TV, listen to the radio, or read the newspaper. They will not tune you out.

The downside of news media coverage is that, unlike any other form of promotion, you have very little, if any, control over the content of your message. Therefore you should look at the opportunities of free media publicity as a supplement to all of your other marketing activities. You can't rely on publicity as a primary means to market your business, but on the other hand, when done properly and in conjunction with all of the other streetsmart marketing programs, it makes an invaluable marketing tool.

Your publicity can be almost anything from a little blurb or mention to a full-feature story. Every time you're mentioned in the media, you create more and more awareness for your business, which in itself helps to bring in new customers while reinforcing regulars. Publicity also helps all of the other streetsmart marketing ideas to work even better.

It may take a number of promotions from different areas before your customer finally takes action. Your future customer gets a "donation dollar" from the local high school candy sale, but stuffs it in a drawer. The next week, she hears your radio commercial. The week after, the local paper carries a story about your business, and a few days later she drives by and sees your front sign. The week after she visits the neighborhood carwash and they hand her a cross-promotion certificate good for savings at your store, and that's when she finally decides to try you.

What one thing finally caused her to try you out? There was no one thing, but a combination of impressions that allowed the final promotion to work. Publicity can add to this effect in a big way.

GETTING READY

One of the most difficult aspects of effective local publicity is forcing yourself to take advantage of it. There are dozens, if not

hundreds, of opportunities every year that can get you free exposure. As mentioned before, it may just be a little blurb in the paper
or a full-feature story. Nevertheless, people do see, read, and hear
these items regardless of their size. They help to create additional
awareness in your community for your business; they also provide
you with other advantages that will be explained later.

DO YOUR HOMEWORK

Before you start getting free publicity, you must first gather
some basic information about all the mass news media that is
available to you and that offer you the potential of getting free
publicity. Prepare a mailing-label master sheet. These usually
come with 33 labels on a standard size of 8 1/2 × 11. With a master list you can photocopy right onto peel-off labels.

On this master label sheet, prepare the labels for mailing by
using every TV and radio station, your local newspapers (dailies
and weeklies), business journals, and local magazines. You may
want more than one label per station or publication. For example,
a TV station has their regular newscast, which is one source. On
that one, you would make your label to the attention of the
newsroom. That same TV station might also have an interview
show, so you want to make a different label for that one.

Your local daily newspaper might have a number of different editors for different sections of the newspaper. You'll learn
later on how to tailor your item for each of them and to make sure
that you have their names, if possible. If it's too much trouble
right now, just put on the address "City Desk" for basic news
items or "attn: Business Editor," "attn: Fashion Editor," or you may
want to send your news item to the "Accent," "Metro," or "Tempo"
editor, depending on what that publication calls their local and
public interest section. There's the "Sports Editor," or perhaps a
"Religion Editor." If you're not sure who is in charge of certain
areas, call the paper and find out about your particular situation.

For a broadcast station, you can usually address it to "News Room, Assignment Editor." For a talk show, you can always send it in care of the show name, then "attn: Producer."

Once you have your label sheet(s) prepared, make one copy on regular paper. Then on each label put the phone number of each contact. That way you have immediate access to either calling or writing that particular news source.

Now that you're prepared, you are ready to act when you get a hot news item. The more prepared you are ahead of time, and the easier you make it for yourself, the more likely you are to take advantage of these great opportunities.

REPORTING NEWSWORTHY NEWS

There are two ways to get a reporter to want to give you publicity: Report a newsworthy story or create a newsworthy story. Sometimes it's a question of which comes first. Many community service programs, for example, lead to free exposure in the media. You would still do those programs even if you didn't get the publicity, yet you need to make the effort for maximum return.

You have two ways to let the media know about your news item. You can either call them on the phone or send something in writing. The written item usually comes in the form of a press release (Figure 5-1). Often you'll call first to see who is really interested, then at their request, you follow up with something in writing. But whether you call or write depends mostly on the news item and the timing of the article.

PRESS RELEASE FORMAT

Using your company letterhead, begin your press release with the contact. That's probably you. It reads, "for further information,

For Further Information Contact:
Gayle Lee
18885 SW Westword St.
Aloha, OR 97007
503/642-2687

Local Oil Changers Help Change Lives

BEAVERTON, OR -- The Oregon chapter of the National Neurofibromatosis (NF) Foundation, (more commonly known as the crippling disease that affected John Merrick, "The Elephant Man"), is sponsoring a major research fund raiser in conjunction with the Beaverton Minit-Lube quick-oil change on Wednesday, August 13th from 8:00 am to 6:00 pm.

On that Wednesday, The National NF Foundation will receive half of the day's profits of those people who get their oil changed at the Beaverton Minit-Lube located at 11150 Beaverton-Hillsdale Highway. According to Dan Johnson, the local NF chapter president, "We hope to raise well over $500, which will go for research to help find a cure for this genetic disorder that affects literally thousands of people right here in Oregon."

"We were first approached by the local NF foundation in a letter asking for our support to help raise the money which is badly needed to research the disease," said Lonnie Brontnov, the store manager of the Beaverton Minit-Lube. "I tried to think of ways that we could help, but at the same time stay within my budget. This seemed like the logical way to go."

NF is a genetic disorder of the nervous system which affects approximately 1 in 4,000 babies born. Although NF can be hereditary, half of all cases are caused by spontaneous gene mutation, meaning any family can be affected. Currently there is no cure.

######

Figure 5-1   The written item usually comes in the form of a press release.

contact," followed by your name, address, and phone. Then a few lines down you'll put "For Immediate Release." Then you need to put a headline on it. This is a few more lines down, centered on the paper, preferably in all caps; and if you have a word processor, put it in bold, as well.

The title is there to catch the reporter's attention. It should be a very brief description of the content of the release and should stress the main point or points. For example, if John Smith gets promoted to vice president of restroom maintenance, then your headline might read, "XYZ COMPANY PROMOTES JOHN SMITH TO VICE PRESIDENT OF RESTROOM MAINTENANCE." Pretty simple, isn't it? Tell them exactly what you have. Don't try to dance around the item. You have a much better chance of getting the item in if you're honest with the reporter. If they don't want your item, nothing you write changes that, so don't waste their time. Also notice that I put the name of the company in the headline. I want the name of my company mentioned in the article.

After the headline, your opening sentence gives all of the major points. Answer the questions who, what, why, where, when, and how in your first sentence. The rest is description.

Keep the release as brief as possible, but include all the important information. The shorter it is, the more likely you are to get it read. If the reporter needs more information, they know where to get in touch with you.

When working with a nonprofit group on a community service program, it works better if the release is done on their letterhead. It looks less commercial that way. Get some letterheads from them, or better yet, have them send the release in. Then they can do all of the work. All you need to do is to guide them in how to structure the release so your company gets major credit in the item.

A single store does not have to be overly sophisticated to get results from the news media. I've seen businesses get great results using simple notes with the critical information to the press. If the item is valid and newsworthy, you'll get the exposure. If it's not, you won't.

One Man's Garbage

It's important not to get caught up in the little details. In the example shown in Figure 5-2 a florist in Indiana got a mention on a couple of radio stations, and he did it by providing free flowers. The free flowers, by the way, were just out of season, and he was going to have to pay $50 to get them hauled away. With this approach, he got people to take them away for him, which introduced his business to many customers and, at the same time, got quite a bit of free radio time plus a blurb in the local paper. He was able to do this by providing the offer to charity groups.

Write or Call

If you have a fairly big news item, you might be better off calling the station or publication on the phone. Tell them exactly what the item is about, but do it in a way that shows some benefit to the reporter. You do not want to call up a reporter and ask them to give you free publicity about your new location, for example. Instead, stress the benefit to the reporter. Talk in terms of the reporters, viewers, readers, or listeners.

For example, when calling a TV station, you might open with something like, "This is Jeff Slutsky, and I have something here I thought your viewers might find interesting." This is very low key and stresses the benefit to the audience.

Then you go on to explain the item. Keep it brief. They don't need a lot of detail. If they're interested, they'll say so. At the end of your brief explanation, end with a question such as, "what do you think?" This asks the reporter to respond to your information so you can see if it's something they want to use.

If your news item if fairly unique, you might have to promise the reporter an exclusive. So you confirm their exclusivity by

BROADVIEW FLORISTS GREENHOUSES, INC.
5409 WINCHESTER ROAD, FORT WAYNE, INDIANA 46819

747-3146

July 1, 1981

FREE PLANTS FOR CHARITY

Broadview Greenhouse has a surplus of
geraniams and bedding plants that they would like
to donate to charitable organizations such as 4-H,
hospitals, nursing homes, city park departments,
etc. . .

For further information please contact
Doug Hackbarth at Broadview Greenhouse. Phone
747-3146

Doug Hackbarth

P.S. Please announce this as many times as
possible between now and July 10th.

1981 Retail Marketing Institute Inc

*It really was
a lovely thought
Thank You
for the joy it brought!*

*Residents of
Lutheran Homes, Inc.
Kendallville*

Figure 5-2 A florist in Indiana got a mention on a couple of radio stations by providing free flowers.

saying, "You will be the only TV station to get this story." By saying it in this way, you can keep your promise to the reporter, but you can also share that same story with one radio station and with one newspaper. Most of the time, when you tell them they'll get an exclusive, they want it for their medium.

There are a few reporters who are arrogant and rude when people suggest stories, but the majority of your local news reporters are very responsive. Remember, they've got a lot of time and space to fill, so they need you as much as you need them. Just don't waste their time with an item that is blatantly a commercial and has no news value. You want to build a rapport with some of the reporters in the area. After awhile, they might come to you about certain stories to get your point of view.

THE NEWS THAT'S FIT TO PRINT

What makes a news item newsworthy? That's hard to say. Much of it depends on which reporter you talk to. Is it a busy news day of a slow news day? What are the hot topics in the news?

First of all, almost every paper prints items like promotions or additions to a company. It's usually just a sentence or two and perhaps a photo. It's not much, but you would be surprised as to how many people read it. So start sending those items in. When we hired our secretary at our main office, we sent a brief press release to the local paper and the weekly business publication. They printed it.

A month later, we promoted her to office manager and sent a press release on that. They printed it. Her duties didn't change, nor her salary; only her title. The next month she was promoted to director of operations. Again, we got a little more press. She got her name mentioned and so did Retail Marketing Institute, our company. In addition to a little exposure, it's a real nice stroke for your employees to see their name in the paper.

Featuring You

Getting a major feature story can be worth its weight in gold. To do it, you need a hook or an angle. Ask yourself, what are you doing that is unique or different that would be of interest to the public? To get an idea of what the press is printing, look at your local paper and watch the TV news carefully. Observe the local merchants who are getting free publicity in your community. What was the angle of the story? Also notice the reporters who covered it. Try to get a feel for the type of stories they like.

If you add a new location, that may be good for a little blurb. But let's say your new location is going to employ 25 people. That might make a nice angle on job opportunities in the local market. What is the reason for your new location? Is there an area of town that is growing fast? That may be the angle you need. Is there anything different about the location itself? Is it the first, newest, oldest, largest, smallest, most beautiful, or ugliest?

We give numerous speeches and seminars each month. That's not newsworthy. But when we were hired to give a seminar in New Delhi, India, we sent in a little press release on it. Sure enough, the business section of the *Columbus Dispatch*, as part of a daily business column, published a paragraph on our trip to India. It was unusual enough to get us some exposure.

Is there anything in local or national current events that would make your item more topical? In one town, citizens started a campaign to picket all the adult bookstores. It was getting a lot of press. This gave us an idea of how to get some attention for an unfinished furniture store. This store was at the corner of the single biggest intersection in the city, yet it was not getting much attention.

The owner of the store told us of a few funny instances where people refused to shop at his store because of the name "Naked Furniture." They thought there might be something obscene about it when, in fact, it was just a clever name for promoting their product—unfinished furniture.

This gave us an idea. To draw some attention to the location, we got a dozen college kids from the local community college to carry picket signs near the street in front of the store. The picket signs had slogans such as "Furniture Yes—People No," "You'll Love Our Drawers," and "See Us Strip."

Naturally, everyone driving by had to pay attention. That in itself made the promotion worth the effort, but we also wanted to get some news exposure. We made phone calls to all the TV and radio stations and the local newspaper. As a result, the number one station in town did a little feature on it in their newscast.

One of the most powerful publicity programs you can do for yourself and your business is to be the local expert on your subject in your community. A regular TV or radio show or a feature column in your local paper can do that for you.

FILM AT 11

After attending our Streetfighting seminar, a florist called the local ABC affiliate TV station and suggested a week-long series on how to care for your house and garden plants. The assignment editor didn't like the idea of a week-long series, but asked him if he would want to do a weekly series on that subject.

Every Tuesday on both the early and the late news, the florist presented a 90-second feature on the various tips for caring for your house and garden plants. This went on for a year and a half. Without a doubt, the florist became known as the premier expert in the plant area. This wasn't a commercial, but they did mention his name and his store.

Customers would come to his store and recognize him as the "guy on TV," and they would buy everything he would recommend because he was the expert. He had tremendous credibility. The local newspaper was doing a feature on the effects of a flood in that market. They had a picture on the front page showing the florist up to his knee caps in the flood waters of his greenhouse and watering all the plants that were elevated on tables. Out of all of the angles they could have taken, for some reason they wanted one that involved plants and this florist. How do you think they came up with that?

After the station discontinued the program, the florist then approached the CBS affiliate that needed a garden and plant related feature for their *PM Magazine* show; they featured the florist for about six months. Then it was back to the ABC affiliate where they needed something on their noon talk show. For three years running, this florist was featured repeatedly and got hundreds of thousands of dollars of free exposure in the local marketplace. He still gets free exposure. It all started with one phone call.

OFF THE RECORD

When talking to a reporter, never say anything "off the record." No matter what a reporter may promise, you are much better off keeping your mouth shut if you don't want what you say in print or broadcast. Don't take the chance.

Sometimes you'll run into reporters who think they are the best. They come to your business with a camera crew, cross, and three nails. Be careful. If the reporter is the one initiating the interview, be sure you get your questions answered before you allow them to tape you.

Ask the reporter what the angle of the story is or what it was that made them want to interview you. You have to find this out and when the story will be aired or published. You also want to know who else they are interviewing.

Some say, "I don't care what they print, as long as they spell my name right." Don't believe it for a second. A negative story can do tremendous harm, and you really have no recourse. If they inaccurately report something negative, you are in trouble. Even if they offer a retraction later, you're still in trouble. Be careful.

PERPETUATING YOUR PUBLICITY

Once you get some publicity, especially in print, make sure that all of your regular customers know about it, because it reinforces that they're dealing with the right business.

Have the article reduced and printed so you can bag stuff it or mail it out with invoices or statements. That's exactly what a travel agency owner did. He received a little blurb in his local paper for claiming top honors at their annual convention for being the highest single-volume agency. He reproduced the paragraph from the paper on a third of a sheet of paper, along with a message that stated, "Thank you for your help in making this happen!!" This nice little reinforcer was placed in the ticket envelopes for a month.

You can also enlarge the article and use it as a display at your location. Or if you have outside salespeople, reproduce it for your presentation materials. It will lend additional credibility to your operation.

◇ Publicity Exercises

1. Make mailing list labels of all the news media in your area.

2. List 10 events in the past 12 months that you think might have made good news stories. What angle would you use with each one? Who would you have contacted in the news media?

3. List 3 events coming up in the near future that would be worth contacting the news media about.

SUMMARY

1. Publicity is great exposure because it's free and credible. It can portray you as the local expert in your field. Your customers have a tendency to remember publicity items more than regular advertising.

2. In approaching a reporter, present your suggestion by stressing the benefits to the reporter's audience.

3. Be prepared. Know all the avenues in your community for getting free publicity, and have a list or mailing labels prepared for each one of them in advance. When a news item happens, call or send it in writing without delay, thus increasing your opportunity of getting free exposure.

4. Begin to look for items that are newsworthy. What do you do that is truly interesting, unusual, or different? Perhaps you can offer a local tie-in to some national story.

Upping Sales on Location

There are three ways in which you can increase your sales: get more customers, get your customers to visit your store more often, and get them to spend more money during their visit.

So far, your focus was primarily on getting new customers, but in this chapter you will work on all three. It's often much easier and more cost effective to get your existing customers to spend more money with you than it is to get new customers, yet this important area is often neglected. As a streetfighter, you must look for every way possible to provide additional service to your customers while adding some extra bucks in the cash register.

CONVERTING EMPLOYEES TO SALESPEOPLE

Contests are a fun way to get your people to do things you want them to do. Increasing sales using a fun contest works well in the area of suggested selling or "up-selling." The reason for pushing the up-sell contest is that once a customer purchases from you, that becomes the easiest way to get more sales. When the customer buys the suit, that's the time to sell the shirts, ties, underwear, and socks. You may find that the up-sale can add as little as an extra 10 percent or as much as double the original sale, depending on what you're selling.

You've often seen up-selling. Examples include the following items:

Rustproofing with the car sale

Wax with the car wash

Cocktails, appetizers, and dessert with dinner

Purse and shoes with a new dress

Fries with a hamburger

Soft drink with fries

Large soft drink rather than small

Air filter with an oil change

Extra coverage with a new million-dollar life-insurance policy

Head cleaner and microwave popcorn with a movie rental

Fish food for your angel fish

Baby's Breath with a dozen roses

Rose-colored tint for your new eyeglasses

Lightbulbs with your duplicate keys (everyone needs light bulbs)

Radiator flush with an oil change

Oil change with a radiator flush

The list is endless. Write down all the extra things that your customers want and need and probably would buy if you suggested that they do so. Make sure that with an add-on sale you sell something that does not get them to change from one main purchase to another, but rather causes them to make an additional purchase of a profitable item.

How you suggest the little something extra can make the difference as well. For example, when a customer is buying something where there are two or three choices, such as the size of a soft drink, do this: instead of saying, "what size?" you would simply say, "large?"

Often your customers want your input. They're not sure which item to buy. Simply suggest the top-of-the-line first, and you will increase your chances of selling it. At the very worst, they'll go down from there. But if you suggest a mid-range item, it's much less likely that your customer will want to step up.

MAKING IT FUN

The "Suggested-Sell Contest" is easy. For a brief period of time, perhaps one week or a month, run a contest with your employees who deal face-to-face with your customers. For the predetermined time, each of those people can win extra money or prizes for up-selling.

Before the contest, make sure your employees understand the item or service you're offering for the contest. Make it just one or two items. Keep your contest very simple. Remember the example in the first chapter of the restaurant owner who had this kind of contest to promote his banana cream pies? The server who sold the most in the month got a free pie to throw in his face. This was very successful and very inexpensive.

One contest that worked well at a pizza restaurant was to see who could sell the most "super supreme" pizzas. Adding extra toppings adds dollars to the bill, and at the same time you're serving a top-of-the-line product. In this case, you're also helping your customers to become accustomed to having the top-of-the-line product, and your chances of helping them get in the habit of ordering it in the future are much better.

I noticed this when I started traveling around the country with great frequency. On a couple of occasions, I got enough bonus points to travel first class. I never realized, prior to that, how much more relaxing the trip is and how much better I did when I arrived at my destination. After a couple of first class trips and then a couple of coach trips, I started traveling first class all the time because the increased level of service was worth it to me. Because of up-selling me initially with a contest, I changed my travel habits. You've probably done the same in certain areas.

NEW CUSTOMERS FROM OLD EMPLOYEES

This next contest combines the effectiveness of testimonial advertising, word-of-mouth, and getting every single employee in your organization to go out there and promote you—free.

The suggested-sell contest is limited to the employees who work directly with your customers, but with the next program you can turn your entire staff into streetfighters, and they'll have fun doing it.

The program is called "The Streetfighter's Employee Referral Contest." You give each one of your employees (both full-time and part-time, and even key suppliers, if you like) 50 special cards (Figure 6-1). When they run out, they can get more. The card entitles your employee's friend to a special savings or value in your location. To really get your employees behind this, it's a good idea to make the value better than a standard coupon or other offers you may have.

When designing your cards, have a signature line on it for the employee to authorize the value. This really strokes your employees' egos. After all, it is management that always hands out special-value cards, and now the employees get to. Also, your

Figure 6-1   Employee referral card.

employees' signatures help to transfer the responsibility of the value to the employee and keeps your business at a distance from the discount or added value. The signature also lets you know which employee is responsible for the redemption so you can keep track and see who wins your contest.

The signature is also a nice touch from the new customers' points of view. Now they know someone on the "inside" who can get them a deal.

You can figure the results in a couple of ways. The easiest is to add up the total number of cards redeemed. The employee who gets the most redemptions wins the first prize. The second highest number of redemptions wins the second prize, and so on all the way down. Everyone who participates should win some kind of prize, even if it's just a $2 car wash.

To get more of the results you want from this contest, consider the winner as the person who generates the most total dollars, not redemptions. As a card is redeemed, attach it to the check or invoice, then track it in terms of total dollars of the sales. This gets your employees thinking about the heavy users they know, not just the buddy who will come in for the deal.

THE RULES

Make the rules very clear to your staff. The contest is voluntary. If they don't want to do it, they don't have to. It's done on their own time, and cards cannot be handed out within the perimeter of the parking lot. You can also say that it's only valid for new customers, but that's difficult to enforce. There are usually one or two employees who will abuse the contest and try to hand them out at your location. Some operators, when they consider that this is a possibility, don't even want to attempt the promotion. There is always a chance that an employee or a customer will take advantage of a situation. You have to do the best you can to anticipate all of the "loopholes" of the promotion, and then close them. And if some still occur, deal with them. The benefits of such a promotion almost always outweigh the little problems that come up.

PRIZES

You don't have to get too fancy with your prizes, but you certainly can offer some nice ones. I prefer, when possible, to trade prizes with other merchants. Movie passes, records, gift certificates at clothing stores, small electronics, free dinners, and t-shirts make great prizes. Before you go in search of these prizes, try to get a very good idea of what kinds of things your staff would really want.

You may want to buy the grand prize. It could be a boom box, a color TV, or a portable radio. Perhaps one of your suppliers has something that would make a great grand prize, such as a free trip for two. Another great prize that has a tremendous perceived value is a day off with pay. Often the day off with pay is a stronger motivator than a prize worth many times its cash value.

Some businesses using this contest put up a little chart in the back room so everyone can see just how they're doing. This is great if everyone is doing about the same, but usually there is one person that does so much better at this than the others that it's probably best to keep the on-going results a mystery. One possibility, however, is to have a weekly grand prize leading up to the grand prize for the entire contest. With the weekly grand prize, after you've won it once, you're not eligible for the next week, but, of course, you can win the over-all. In this way, you can keep a number of your staff motivated to get out there and hand out those cards or certificates.

CLONING YOUR CUSTOMERS

Now that you have your employees out there street-fighting, you can run a similar contest with your regular customers. The customer referral program can be extremely powerful for you because it combines the testimonial of a satisfied customer with the free distribution of a cross promotion. Since you should have many hundreds of customers to work with, the results, if done properly, can be very dramatic.

The reason most businesses don't get as many referrals from their customers as they should is because they don't ask for them. Even when you ask your customers to tell their friends about you, it's not enough. Your customers need both an incentive and a reminder to refer you to their friends.

The "buddy pass" (Figure 6-2) is used in businesses that are service-oriented, such as health clubs, tennis or racquetball clubs, hair salons, warehouse clubs, karate or judo schools,

```
┌─────────────────────────────────────────────────────────────────┐
│                          Guest Pass                               │
│            ALL SPORTS FITNESS CENTER                              │
│                                                                   │
│                 Name _____            │
│       (Nautilus logo)                                             │
│                 Phone _____            │
│                                                                   │
│                 This pass entitles the above person to 50% off    │
│                 one introductory week (valued at $19.50, a        │
│                 savings of $9.75). Good for up to three visits.   │
│                                                                   │
│                 Compliments of _____     │
│                                                                   │
│                                                                   │
│                              Offer Expires_____/_____/_____    │
│     3602 SOUTH CALHOUN (Across from South Side) • (219) 456-1956  │
│         OPEN SIX DAYS A WEEK • CALL FOR AN APPOINTMENT             │
└─────────────────────────────────────────────────────────────────┘
```

Figure 6-2   Buddy pass.

gymnastic schools, and weight control and other behavior-modification classes, but this can be adapted to just about any type of business.

With the buddy pass, you get your existing members or customers to distribute the special pass that is good for a few free introductory visits. The purpose is to get them interested enough in what you have that they'll want to join the organization and will pay full price to do so.

When people first become your customers, they are usually at their peak of excitement of buying from you. At that time, you give them a small number of special passes or certificates (perhaps three passes to begin with) to give to their friends. You tell them that for everyone who uses the pass and buys from you (rents an apartment, buys a membership, leases a car, etc.), they get a reward.

The strongest reward is cash. You can also offer things such as extra months or some added values you may have, but usually cash works the best. Since you only pay it when you have the paid order, there is no risk. Depending on the investment, you can give them anywhere from $5 to $100 to get their attention. And if they need more cards, you make them available.

The value of the card that your customers pass out can be anything you want. It should have just a strong enough value to get your customers' attention without jeopardizing your profit margin. The offer has to be better than any advertised special that anyone off the street can get if you want your customers to feel good about giving you this free exposure.

Part of the effectiveness is that you are giving your customers printed referral cards that have a value. Without something tangible in their hands, such as these cards, your results will be substantially reduced. Because the card has value, your customer has a reason to hand it to a friend.

THE BUDDY-PASS CONTEST

This is the type of promotion that you can do on an ongoing basis with new customers. But to bring new life into your existing customers, once a year you can run a big contest. They still get their prize for each sale, but in addition, the person who brings in the most sales can win a trip or a TV or something else of value. The value might be anywhere from $250 to $1000, again depending upon how much cash you intend to generate from this effort.

You also want to have some runner-up prizes. Second and third place should be decent. Also have consolation prizes for everyone. You can put a minimum requirement to qualify for any of the big prizes. For example, they have to have no less than three friends who have signed leases for apartments before they are even eligible to go after any of the top three prizes. This protects you in case only one person brings in one new customer.

This can add excitement during a slower time of the year,

and it turns your business' biggest asset—your customers—into a bigger asset.

GETTING YOUR CUSTOMERS TO BOUNCE BACK

Getting your customers to increase their number of visits to you is another way to increase sales, as was mentioned in the beginning of this chapter. How do you do it? You have to give them a reason to use you more. To illustrate this, think about a product you should be familiar with, such as baking soda. I assume this product is used in baking. The only time I ever used it was in my third-grade science class. We combined it with vinegar in a small plastic bag so it would explode.

Then another use was promoted for this product: open the box and stick it in your refrigerator for a few months. Then remove the box and dump it down the drain. Brilliant! I can't remember how many times I've seen refrigerators containing a box of baking soda. Even the small refrigerator at the office has one in it. A new need was created for an old product. That's what you need to do.

Find out why customers shop with you and find one more reason for them to shop more often. If you have a restaurant, you can get your dinner customers to come for lunch, your lunch customers to come for breakfast, or your breakfast customers to use your catering services. If your customer buys his suits from you, then you may want that customer to consider your store for casual clothes. Do they use your health facilities but don't rent your tennis or racquetball courts or sign up for classes? There are any number of other products and services you can offer to your customers.

One way to do this is to use a "Bounce Back" certificate. This is one of the few times it makes sense to use an internal "coupon," because you're asking them to come back for another reason (Figure 6-3).

Another time when it make sense to use an internal coupon is when you're doing a special promotion that is attracting a lot of first-time customers. Many of your major community involvement programs do this, and since these people are trying you out under special circumstances, you can invite them to visit with you again under more normal circumstances. Plus, since these community involvement events are in conjunction with a local nonprofit group, you can make your internal certificate compliments of them. This will further protect your price credibility.

You don't even have to offer a discount if you don't want to. Pass out, bag stuff, or envelope stuff a message about other services or products you offer to constantly remind your customers of all the benefits of buying from you. Always look for inexpensive opportunities to communicate with your customers.

FORTIFYING WITH FREQUENCY PROMOTIONS

Many businesses run various types of promotions where you get some reward for buying a certain number of items. You often see this with punch cards. This can be a powerful promotion if done right.

The time to use this type of program is when you anticipate a problem. Perhaps after Christmas your sales drop for awhile. That would be the time to run a frequency promotion like a punch card. Your offer could be "buy five and the sixth one is free."

Plan your promotion so that the majority of your customers get their free one at the beginning of the anticipated down time. If it is after Christmas, for example, you might start your punch card the first of November. By the time Christmas arrives, they're just one purchase away from their freebie. That's strong enough

Dear Minit-Lube Customer,

Thank you for coming to our Grand Opening Celebration. We hope you like our service and will give us the opportunity of serving you again in the near future. Save this special "Thank You" certificate for your next visit and you'll save $2.

Sincerely,

Steve Loski
Manager

Good only at the following Minit-Lube® locations:

521 N.E. 181st • 665-7303
On the Corner of 181st & Glisan
Across from Pay 'N Pak

No Appointment Necessary

Figure 6-3   Bounce back from special event.

to get them to come back in the first week of your down time. Then the following week, they come in for their freebie. You are now two weeks into your troubled time, but you've kept the momentum going. It's now less likely that those particular customers will take a small vacation from you.

Another time to use the frequency promotion is when you have a competitor opening up near you. You want to plan your promotion so that the strongest incentive goes head-to-head with their grand opening. If you know that their grand opening is June 1, you start your "buy four get the fifth free" promotion on May 7. By June 1, your customers are just one purchase away from getting their freebie. That buys you two weeks of sales into their grand opening.

COMPETITIVE ENTRY

While on the subject of competition, you need to develop a strategy to deal with someone trying to take over your turf. Most businesses just wait until the new competitor has had their day in the sun, then they catch up later. Wrong. You go head-to-head with that new competitor. Go after that grand opening.

Granted, a grand opening is something that attracts a lot of people, many of whom are your customers. Even so, you do everything you possibly can to steal every possible dollar away from that opening.

The reason for this is because most businesses use their grand opening as a barometer of how well they think they'll do at that location. If they do $10,000 per week during the first month of their opening, their anticipation then might be to settle in at 80 percent of that, or $8000 per week or $416,000 for the year.

Use every promotion you can think of to keep customers from going to that new store, such as frequency, cross promotions, community service, publicity, sidewalk sales, strong media, anniversary sales, and so on. This is the one time you pull out all of the stops. This is one time you forget the "one-at-a-time/one-week-at-a-time" rule. This is a rumble—a gang war! Every dollar you can steal away reduces their anticipated annual revenue. In the example above, if you could steal away just $1000 a week that first month and reduce their grand opening sales from $10,000 to $9000, then their anticipated annual revenue would settle in at 80 percent (or whatever percentage they use) of the lower amount. That would be $7200 per week or $374,400 per year. They would anticipate making about $41,000 less a year, which makes your job easier.

SIGNS SELL

Signs in your store really help to sell more merchandise. The right kind of signs add excitement to the store and interest to the product. It doesn't necessarily have to be a price-related sign. You can promote benefits which help presell the item before the sales person gets to the customer.

A video rental store, for example, can add a great deal of interest about certain titles if, on a sign, it was mentioned that a certain actor is in it or it won an academy award (Figure 6-4).

Get some of the regular customers to write quotes about certain products or services you have. Type up those quotes on $5^{1}/_{2} \times 8^{1}/_{2}$ cards and display them near the merchandise. This is a powerful selling tool.

Look for places at your location to communicate with your customers. Use wall frames for posters, table tents, badges, counter cards, register displays, danglers, banners, or balloons. If you have something to say to customers, say it so that they know what you have.

When working with a pizza restaurant, we knew we had a captive audience for about 20 minutes before the dinner arrived.

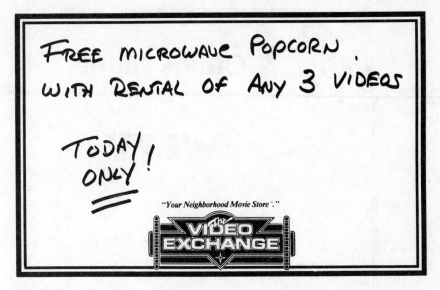

Figure 6-4 Customized blank sign cards make it easy for you to communicate new information to your customers.

The placemat became a major advertising tool. When I invested in a nightclub a few years later, I used a similar idea. Instead of expensive cocktail napkins, we had customized inexpensive coasters that were printed at the local quick printer. This allowed us to promote all kind of items, and every time someone ordered a drink, the coaster was placed in front of them. We went through so many that companies offered to pay us or give us free merchandise for our contest to get their name mentioned on the coaster (Figure 6-5).

THE INTERNAL PROMOTION YOU NEVER USE!

Many times I see various retail businesses with a free drawing from a local health club. You get to give away a free membership to one of your customers and the health club gets leads. Everyone wins, right? No way. There is a real danger with this

Figure 6-5   Beverage coaster-turned-promotional medium.

type of promotion and, for that reason, I'll never let anyone do a free drawing from my place.

The reason is simple. What if your competition got that list? Your customer list is the most important thing you have. Look at it another way. How would you take advantage of a customer list of one of your competitors?

StreetSmart Research

Where do your customers come from? That is easy to find out. Do your own free drawing. On the entry blank have a line for name, address, phone, and maybe some other information such as place of employment and occupation. After the drawing is over, take the entry forms (which make a great mailing and telephone list) and plot the addresses on a map. Get a map of your area and a box of push pins and plot where your customers live or work, depending on where they're coming from. This gives you a good idea as to what areas you need to promote.

If you see a big bald spot on your map that shouldn't be there, first find out why. Is there a major barrier in the way, such as a highway, railroad tracks, or a bridge? People have a tendency not to cross such barriers. Or you may have a major competitor in that area. This helps to give you a birds-eye view of your customers so you can plan where to work your promotions.

One of the more interesting StreetSmart research techniques was used by a car wash. They wanted to find out what radio station their customers listened to most. So, for one month, the attendant who cleaned the inside would look at the station the car was tuned to and mark it on a tally sheet. This was inexpensive, and it gave them a good idea of the stations they should buy advertising from.

FIND OUT WHAT THEY *REALLY* THINK OF YOU

An easy way to get an idea of how your community feels about your business is to use the "I'm new in town" approach. If people in your neighborhood will recognize you, then you may want to get a friend to do this for you, and you can return the favor.

Go to a few businesses, such as a local gas station. Tell the attendant, "I'm new in town. Can you recommend a good place to go for pizza?"

You'll probably get a few suggestions. If one of those suggestions is *not* your place, follow up with, "I thought I remembered seeing a 'Jeff's Pizza & Subs.' What about that place?" You should get some good insight as to your perception from people in your neighborhood.

TRACKING THE RESULTS OF YOUR ADVERTISING

You need to know which ads work and which ads waste money so you can fine tune your advertising efforts to get a better return on your investment. To get a fairly decent indication as to which advertising medium is generating customers, simply ask them. When you get someone into your business, ask, "by the way, how did you hear about us?" Then have a tally sheet with all the possible sources you have for generating new customers. Your list may include TV, radio, newspaper, magazine, Yellow Pages, billboards, walk-in, front sign, and referrals. If it is a referral, ask who referred them.

After you've done this for a period of time, you'll start to get a good indication of what's working. You'll also find that the more money you throw into a certain medium, the more response you'll get from it.

Another thing you can do with your print advertising, if your customer response is initially a phone call, is to print an extension number next to your phone number. Then when the customer calls up and you ask them what extension, you know exactly which ad was responsible for the call. Let's say you run a newspaper ad three times a week. On Tuesday your extension in the ad is 12, on Thursday it's 13, and on Sunday it's 14. When they tell you the extension number, you know exactly which ad it was that got your response.

All of this activity is designed so you can begin to eliminate the ads that aren't pulling their weight. There are a number of variables of any ad that you have to consider. The medium you chose is just the beginning. The size of the ad is also important.

In print you may measure it in column inches or lines, while in broadcast it might be in 10-, 15-, 30-, 60- and 90-second segments. Outdoor advertising is another issue.

The frequency of the ad, the media mix, and the content or creative aspects of your ad are also important variables. It can get complicated. But once you start advertising, test and track your ads so you can make modifications.

FOCUSING ON YOUR CUSTOMERS

Another inexpensive form of advertising is the informal focus group. Gather together about six to eight of your customers for a group session. Perhaps you can buy them lunch. Then start asking them to make suggestions on ways to make your business better in their eyes. Let them do the talking, and don't offer solutions. This a fact-gathering and eye-opening session for you.

You may have to ask a few questions to get the customers talking. When you ask your questions, use open-ended questions that require explanation. These are questions that begin with who, what, why, where, how, and when. Stay away from questions that can be answered with a yes or a no.

For example, you could ask, "Is there anything we can do to make our business better?" They could then respond by saying it's okay as it is. But instead you could ask, "What are three areas where you think we could use some improving?" Then ask, "Why?" This is also a good place to practice the echo technique you learned about in Chapter 2.

Remember, this is not meant to be an ego-stroking session for you. You know what you're doing right. This is to give you more ideas on how you can be even better.

This technique can even be done one-on-one or in smaller groups. You decide where you feel comfortable, then get the information you need to better serve your customers.

BLOW THEM AWAY WITH A REAL BLOW-OUT

In his now classic book on advertising, *From Those Wonderful Folks Who Brought You Pearl Harbor,* Jerry Della Femina tells the story of the early days of his Madison Avenue Advertising Agency. In short, it was about to go under. Broke. Bankrupt. Chapter 11.

Rather than just fade away gracefully, Jerry and his partners decided to give it one last shot and either turn the agency around or really go out in style. Taking their last $10,000, they sunk it into the biggest agency party New York had seen in years. They invited every client and potential client they could think of.

It worked! The struggling agency began to turn around. It not only worked for Jerry Della Femina, but we've seen it work for dozens of types of local businesses over the years.

For example, when a nightclub I had a stake in opened its doors, we fought to keep them open for months. We did various types of advertising and some promotions, but it was a new club on a side of town that didn't usually have such clubs. It was tough. Then a local radio station decided to throw a party for their listeners. They wanted to give away free beer and wine all night long. We volunteered our club and alcohol to do the promotion. By 9:00 P.M., the club was full. This was never before seen by us. By 10:00 P.M., there was a waiting line half way around the building. It was the one single event that turned the place around from a loser to the number one club in the city.

A huge pizza restaurant that had a bad location ran a pizza special—"all the pizza you can eat for only 99¢." Despite the below-zero temperature and the blizzard the day before, they created such a traffic jam that the state police had to come out to direct traffic.

The "Blow-Out" promotion is a major event, unlike setting up a cross promotion or a community service event. It's a very powerful promotion that has to be planned just right; otherwise, it could backfire on you. However, it can be the single promotion that can really get the ball rolling for you. For a new store or one that has had problems in the past, this is your one chance to get new customers to try you out. But if you screw it up, you'll lose them forever!

When teaching this particular technique, it is interesting to see the reactions of the various businesspeople. Some immediately get excited, while others are violently opposed. They can't understand why they would ever give their product away.

Think of it this way: By using mass advertising media, how much would it cost you, out of pocket, to create enough impact to bring in hundreds of new customers? Depending on your market, you could be spending thousands upon thousands of dollars, and even then there are no guarantees that the people will show.

But, if for just one or two days, you took your best product or service and sold it at a ridiculously low price, they would come out of the woodwork for it. Even though you lost money on the sale of that item, figure in the value of getting a new customer in the door the first time.

There are 10 guidelines for not blowing the blow-out:

1. *"Legit" low price*
   You need a price point that is low enough to draw a good crowd, but you also have to deliver a good product and a fun time for the promotion to be super effective. The price must be ridiculously low. The purpose is not to generate profit for this product right now, but to generate trial and exposure to get those people in the front door for the first time so that they see what you have to offer.

2. *A narrow time frame*
   Part of the magic seems to be because these promotions are held in a very short time period, such as one or two days.

3. *Full preparation*

People are usually forgiving as far as waiting in line if the deal is a good one. But make sure that you have plenty of inventory. Nothing is worse than promoting something that is too good to be true and then run out of the product. This will cause far more harm than good. Also, make sure that you give the customers exactly what you advertised. Put your best foot forward. Don't give them the watered-down version, but the top-of-the-line. This is your opportunity to show them exactly what you have.

Also make sure that you have plenty of staff. Bring people in from other locations if need be, but have them there. You'll need one person just to answer the phones and another possibly to direct traffic.

4. *Limited advertising expenditures*

You don't have to spend a lot of money on advertising— just enough to get the word out. You also want to start advertising only three or four days before your promotion. Advertising further in advance will kill your regular sales.

5. *Bounce them back*

Give your new customers a reason to visit you again, but under more normal circumstances. Use a bounce-back certificate that thanks them for coming to your party or celebration and that has an offer for when they return. Since this is part of a special event, you don't have to worry about hurting your regular price credibility.

6. *A party atmosphere*

Plan some party events during your promotion. Decorate the place with balloons, streamers, and so on. Your staff can wear special hats or t-shirts. You could hire a clown, magician, mime, polka band, or anything that makes this event feel special. You might get a radio station's remote broadcast package for this. Though you really won't need all of the exposure, it would get the word out for you quickly, and the live call-ins and having a local radio celebrity on hand adds to the party atmosphere.

7. *A free drawing*
It not only adds to the festivities, but you'll have a very important mailing/telephone list for follow-up marketing efforts. The give-away isn't really important, but it should be strong enough to get everyone to enter. You want their name, phone, address, work phone, work address, and you can even ask two or three research questions.

8. *An inventory of regular-priced goods*
Even though it's a party, there's nothing wrong with making a few bucks. So have plenty of other merchandise available for sale. Your blow-out item is the only thing priced that low. Get full mark-up on all of the other items. This helps you to recover some of the loss margins.

9. *A good reason for your promotion*
It is your birthday or your anniversary, or your softball team won the regionals. You need a reason for the party.

10. *One store at a time*
If you have more than one store in the marketplace, only do the promotion with one of them. You want the waiting lines and the craziness. Some people will drive by, all set for what you have, and then see the line and travel across town to another of your locations and pay full price.

The blow-out is something you can do once or twice a year. Test a few different price points, but when you do it, make sure the price is low enough to create the impact you want.

Your other internal marketing contests are also done once or twice a year. Mix them in with all of your other promotions and community service projects, and your year is filled with a variety of promotions that effectively network you into your community.

StreetSmart Tele-Selling and Mail with Moxie

Two of the most valuable *streetsmart marketing* assets that you have at your fingertips are often overlooked by many businesses. They are the customers who have bought from you in the past and customers who are considering buying from you in the near future. Both of these groups are prime targets for getting new sales easily because they have already expressed interest in your business.

The biggest hurdle in marketing is getting a customer to first express an interest in coming to your shop. Businesspeople think nothing of spending a small fortune to reach the masses just to create enough interest to get them to visit or call. Yet, if you harvest your efforts, you will have many of these people ready to buy from you.

It takes you a fraction of the effort and the money to get these two groups to buy from you. To reach the former buyers and the shoppers, you need to know how to effectively use the telephone and the mail. In this chapter, you'll learn some simple and easy techniques for getting results from both.

NEVER LET THEIR FINGERS DO THE WALKING

The telephone can be your best friend or your worst enemy. You must make the right choice, because it won't be neutral. Your potential customers have been brainwashed by the Yellow Pages to get them to call first before they shop in your store. From a business point of view, it's the worst possible situation.

First of all, the Yellow Pages is perhaps the only major advertising medium that surrounds your ad with that of all of your competitors. So you certainly *don't* want to put in your regular advertising, "Look at our Yellow Pages ad."

When a potential buyer calls your business, they usually ask you a few questions. Most of those questions relate to the *availability* and *price* of a certain product or service. Once they know you have what they want and the cost of it, they call a dozen other places. Then they make their decision, which is usually based on the lowest price. Most of the time, you've never even had the opportunity to show them the advantages of what you have to offer.

By turning telephone shoppers into on-site shoppers or by making an appointment for an in-home demonstration, you increase your chances of a sale dramatically. An apartment complex was able to turn around its sales by doing this. After a review of the telephone and traffic logs for the past few months, it was clear that they had a reasonably large number of phone calls and a small number of on-site visits. Most of the on-site visits, by the way, were walk-ins who did not make an initial phone call.

Prior to the visit, a little streetsmart research was done. A couple of different calls were made to the property asking, "How much is a one bedroom apartment?" The woman on the other end of the line responded with, "$325, and that includes your heat." The callers thanked her and hung up.

Right away the problem was clear. Inquiry calls were

made, which means that they were more qualified as a potential customer than the average person on the street. She allowed them to hang up without getting a name, address, phone number, or even finding out if they were interested in stopping by. That's a valuable lead that, more than likely, will be lost to the competition.

The first thing we did to turn it around was to make it very clear to everyone handling the phones at this businesses what the objectives of a telephone inquiry are. There are three:

1. *Qualify*
   You must make sure that the person you're talking to has the potential of being a paying customer. If they don't, you certainly don't want to waste your time. Depending on your type of business, you may find that they must pass six different tests before they qualify. If they fail any one, you're wasting your time.

2. *Set Up the Appointment*
   These customers don't do you any good if they don't come to visit you at your business or invite you to visit them. You may not even require appointments, but it doesn't matter. The purpose of setting up the appointment is to create an emotional *commitment* on the part of your prospect to visit with you. Once they have a specific day and time set up, your chances of them showing up are much greater than if you just have them show up anytime.

3. *Get Their Name, Address, Phone*
   This is a good lead. They called you and that makes them potentially valuable. If for some reason you can't get them to come to you, make sure you have a way of getting in touch with them. Creating this phone and mailing list becomes one of the most valuable assets in your business.

HELPING THEM MAKE THE RIGHT CHOICE

Getting the customer from the phone to the facility is easy once you start following a few simple steps and understand what motivates these people.

The first step is to *get control of the conversation.* You'll remember from earlier chapters that this is done by asking questions. The person who asks the questions is in control of the conversation. So you have to be asking the questions, not answering them.

Let's use our apartment complex for an example. The customer calls up and asks, "How much is your one bedroom apartment?"

At this point, your customer is in ⌐ ⌐⌐ ' If you answer that question right away, especially with a sp   c price, your customer doesn't need your help anymore. They   'l the information they need to make a decision, and they,   ⌐ ⌐bt, will make the wrong one. After all, how can they poss⌐   ⌐nder-stand that your rooms are bigger and the buildings are safer unless they see it for themselves?

You gain control of the conversation by responding with a logical question. We used, "When would you be needing it?"

Right away we are in control. The lead is giving us information we need to know so we can begin to qualify as well. Plus, by asking questions, we are perceived by them as empathetic and caring about their needs.

If they responded with, "I won't be needing it until next year," then you know you do not have a good lead because they are not in a position to buy. For this project, we had six different tests or qualifiers that they had to pass before we considered any lead qualified. They were:

1. *Need*

    They had to need an apartment. If they had just signed a lease with someone else a month prior and were already thinking about moving, we couldn't get that person to commit to us in a reasonable amount of time; to be practical, we had to assume that this lead was unlikely to buy from us.

2. *Want*
They may need an apartment, but may not want what we have. Perhaps they're looking for something on a different side of town than where we're located and would not consider anything in our area. If so, why waste our time?

3. *Decision maker*
Is the person you're talking to the one who will sign the lease? If not, you're wasting your time. You want the actual decision maker there. In the apartment situation, there were a great deal of dual decision makers. You need both of them at the same time in order to get the sale.

4. *Decision mode*
Are they in a position to make a decision? You may have a decision maker there, but if that decision maker is not willing to commit, for whatever reason, you're again wasting your time. If they're not even ready to move for six months, they're not in a position to make a decision. We notice this a great deal when talking with meeting planners for conventions. The person we're talking to can sign the contract, but their event is nine months off and they don't even begin planning for their speakers until three months before the program. At that point, we put them in a tickler file because there is nothing we can do to get a decision in the near future.

5. *Budget*
Can this person afford and are they willing to pay for what you have? If they can't, blow them off. Find out if they can while you have them on the phone. Whenever

you give someone a price on the phone or in person, you always follow up with the question, "Is that in your budget?" or "Is that in the ballpark?" Invite the response. If it's not and we know about it, we can't help these people. Also, try not to give specific prices on the phone at all if you can avoid it. If you must give a price, give them a range and keep it as ambiguous as possible.

When they ask, for example, "How much is the one bedroom?" you might respond with, "Our units range between $325 and $450, depending on which style best suits your needs. Would that be in your budget?" Also, when giving a price, you don't want to say, "325 dollars." Just give the numbers without the dollars. On the other hand, if this particular deal saves them money, you do use dollars. "This unit is 325, which saves you $25 over our other model."

If they can't afford your low end, this is the time to find out. But if this question doesn't disqualify them, you know another important piece of information.

6. *Credit*
   This one is obvious. If they don't have the credit, or if there is a good chance that their credit application is going to be denied, you have the option to see if they can get a co-signer or figure out if it's worth your while to pursue it.

Your qualifiers may be different. You may want to use only a few of these and add others of your own. The purpose of these qualifiers is not to close the customers on the phone, so keep them basic. The main purpose in this is to make sure you don't get hit with any hidden surprises that can blow the sale after you've spent all that time showing the customer everything you have to offer.

The people in your business that answer the phones need a survey sheet or prompt sheet they can follow; once they have a lead on the line, they can easily follow this procedure. Below is an example of the survey sheet used by an apartment complex. Try to keep it from one to one-and-a-half pages. Leave spaces between questions so you can write the answers on the sheet. Have a stack of these by each phone.

Lakewood East Telephone Inquiry Sheet

Date: _____ Time: _____ Name: _____

1. We're glad you called Lakewood East. How can I help you?

2. Is this for yourself? (Who else will be living with you?)

3. How soon do you need to move in?

4. Our units range from 325 to 465, depending on the style that best suits your needs. Is this within your budget?

5. Great. By the way, my name is (first and last name). And whom am I speaking to?

6. Well (first name), let me ask you this—other than yourself, who else would you want to consult with before you decide where you want to move?

7. I see. And where are you living now?
   Really. Why are you considering leaving there?
   No kidding. How long have you been there?

8. Uh ha. Where else have you looked?

9. What is it about (place looked) that really got your attention? I see.

10. What's the one thing about (place looked) that you would change if you could?

11. By the way, how did you hear about Lakewood East?

12. Would we be convenient to your job?

Great. Where do you work?

Really. What type of work do you do?

How long have you been there? How do you like it there?

13. You know, (first name) it sounds to me as though Lakewood East might have just what you're looking for. Let me suggest this. I would like to set up a time when you could come in and visit with us. This would give you an opportunity to see exactly what we have to offer you. I would be glad to personally show you around and answer all your questions so you can make an intelligent decision about us. Fair enough?

14. Super! What would be the best time for you? Later today, or would tomorrow be better? Great. What's a good time for you? (Find out the time they want and set it within 10 minutes of that time).

15. Great. (first name) please spell your last name for me. And your telephone number? And your current mailing address?

16. Thank you (first name), we're all set up for (day) at (time). If for some reason you can't make it, please give me a call so we could reserve that time for someone else. Okay?

17. Oh, (first name), before I let you go, let me ask you one other thing. Who else do you know who is looking for an apartment in the near future? Really. Why do you suggest him/her?

Who else do you know?

18. Great. I appreciate your help. I promise I'll get in touch with (friend's name) right away. When I do, is there any reason why I shouldn't mention your name? Great. Thank's again (first name), and I'll be looking forward to meeting you in person on (day). Take care.

You'll notice that each one of those questions has a specific purpose and, once completed, you have a great deal of information about the prospective buyer. Most people who call answer every single one of the questions. When we first start such programs, the participants just don't believe that customers will answer all of those questions, but a surprising number of them do. Of course, there are always a few who are rude. It happens, but it's not important.

Notice that question 17 asks for a referral. The best time to get a referral is right then, before they become your customer. Referrals are one of the best sources of good qualified leads. Our own customers, and even potential customers, are a tremendous reservoir of new sales.

Practice and role play with this sheet over and over again. Also have people calling a couple of times a week to make sure your phone people are doing it right. If you have a receptionist or secretary answering your calls, transfer that responsibility to your salespeople. They know that we have these mystery callers, but they don't know when they're going to call, so they're always on their toes. It works great, and after awhile this entire approach becomes a habit.

Now you have to adapt this concept to your business. It may not be appropriate for a fast food restaurant, but it can and has been used in a variety of businesses, including a karate school, a health club, a condo conversion project, numerous apartment complexes, a quick oil change, caterers, and others. Even traditional retail-type places such as clothing stores, jewelry stores, shoe stores, department stores, and electronics and appliance stores can adapt this program. Tell them that you want to make sure you'll be there to help them personally. The point is that you want them to make that commitment to visit your store whether you usually have appointments or not.

If you have the type of business where potential customers call up for information and it would be to your advantage to see them face-to-face, then this program will work for you.

PRO-ACTIVE CALLING

You don't have to wait for the phone to ring to get customers. It's easy to develop a simple telemarketing program that can get you in touch with your customers so that you either close them right on the phone or set up an appointment to close them in person. Your approach depends largely on the type of product or service you offer.

An outgoing tele-selling program works best when you're calling customers you already know. Start with your own customer list. This particular approach might be used as a low-cost alternative to an expensive direct mail campaign. Remember, the vast majority of mail gets tossed in the trash, and you pay for the postage whether it is read or not.

BRINGING THEM BACK IN THE FOLD

Start by going over a list of customers you haven't seen in awhile. There must be a reason why they stopped coming to your store. You also may find that with a simple call or note, you can get them back. The gentleman who cuts my hair told me that he had 19 former customers he hadn't seen in awhile. He took his business card and on the back wrote, "I miss you." He then mailed out the 19 cards. Six people called him and made appointments! Not only did he get a nice return on his little investment, but when you project out what a good customer is worth to him over the next few years, that's quite a bit of money.

Now figure out how much it would have cost him to generate six *new* customers. Step two is to call the remaining 13 who did not respond. He got another four appointments!

Calling your regular customers is often perceived as a real service. There's a small women's clothing chain in the midwest. Once a salesperson there helps you, you become her client forever. She keeps a file card on you with your size, style preferences, and some general background information such as your children's names and ages, husband's name, anniversary date, birthdates, and so on. This information is gathered over several visits and kept on simple index cards.

When a new line comes in, the salespeople are on the phone (some send out handwritten notes in the mail) letting their customers know what they have and putting aside their size for them. If a certain dress or coat goes on sale and they know you've had your eye on it, you get a phone call. Your birthday is coming up, so your husband gets a call to let him know that you've had your eye on a certain evening gown, and with his American Express card number on file, she could ship it gift-wrapped to him in plenty of time for your birthday. (You can imagine how many grateful husbands there are as a result!)

Leave no stone unturned. By letting the customer know that you have a solution to their problem, you get the sale. That problem may be finding the perfect graduation gift, anniversary gift, and so on.

Now ask yourself how you can adapt this concept to your business. It doesn't matter if you sell pizzas, pens, puppies, or paintings; an active tele-selling program will increase your sales for your existing customers while improving the new customers you get from word-of-mouth and referrals.

You can conduct your telephone selling efforts and/or direct mail efforts with greater ease using some of the popular computer programs.

Instead of keeping all of your clients on index cards for example, you merely plug them into the computer. They offer several ways of identifying clients—whether by name, business, or even the specific products or services they buy from you.

Let say for example you run a shoe store. You get a shipment of AAA pumps in different colors. Your computer would record the shoe size and preferred styles of your better customers.

With this program, you simply tell the computer you want those customers who wear AAA and have expressed an interest in pumps. Perhaps 55 customers are selected. Once sorted, you can either send them a personalized letter or card with the built in word processor or simply, with a keystroke, the computer dials the number, and provides with a little script or outline that informs those you've called of the fabulous selection of shoes in their size. It makes the pro-active telephone sales effort easier and faster plus nothing is lost between the cracks again. We'll discuss one such program that we found particularly useful in Chapter 9.

REAPING FROM REFERRALS

Once you get a referral, you need to follow up and convert that referral into a new customer. You follow the same prompt sheet as before, but your opener is just a little different.

"Mr. Smith, this is Jeff Slutsky with the Retail Marketing Institute. I promised John Jones that I would give you a call to tell you about our "Streetfighting" program. John said that you might be interested in learning how to advertise, promote, and increase sales without spending a lot of money. Any reason why you wouldn't want to learn a little about it?"

In the opener of your phone call, you need to state who you are and the purpose of your call. Don't waste their time with insignificant details. You also need to say that you promised their friend that you would call. This helps to break down the barriers.

When you state the purpose of your call, do it in a way that stresses benefits. In the example above that we use in our office, we do not say we conduct seminars and consulting on local store marketing. That means nothing. Instead, we convey the *benefit* of the program: "how to advertise, promote, and increase sales without spending a lot of money." This gets their attention.

Then you conclude by asking a question to get in control but you don't ask any type of question; you ask a *negative* question. When most people get a phone call, their natural response is to say "no." So, why fight it. We want them to say "no," but we ask the question in such a way that when they say "no," they're actually giving us an affirmative answer to our question, thus permitting you to continue your presentation.

Tele-selling, whether pro-active (you call) or re-active (they call you), is helpful to any type of business. Even businesses that you normally would not think would benefit from these programs really can. You may run a department store or a flower shop. When customers call about availability or price, go through the survey form. Qualify them and set up the appointment. Even if you don't make appointments at your store, get their commitment to show up. If possible, get the sale over the phone and ship it to them. Use that phone. For more on tele-selling, refer to *The 33 Secrets of StreetSmart Tele-Selling* listed in the Resource Guide.

MAILING WITH MOXIE

Direct-mail advertising is a major advertising medium. On a local level, there's a great deal you can do with the mail to increase sales on a limited budget. Mail advertising can be very expensive, yet it can be very effective. In the remainder of this chapter, you'll focus on some simple mailing ideas that are inexpensive and get results.

POSTCARD MAILING

The biggest problem with direct mail is that 95 percent of it is trashed before it even gets read. If you're going to mail advertising, think of some ways that will cause your customers to read it before they trash it. That's exactly what one smart quick printer did. She was at a printer's convention in Las Vegas. While she was there, she bought 400 picture postcards of the city showing the exciting bright lights of the casinos.

She brought back those cards and on the reverse side printed, "Don't Gamble with Your Printing. Bring this card in for a 10 percent savings on your next order." She had her kids hand address them using the bold face listings of businesses she did not recognize as being her customers from the neighborhood phone book.

She received 100 of them back! That's a 25 percent response, which is unheard of. The reason is because most junk mail is thrown away. On the other hand, if you get a picture postcard from someone, you're going to read the back to see who it's from.

A person who owned a garage was in Orlando visiting Disneyworld. He brought back postcards with headlines that read, "Don't Mickey Mouse Around with Your Car."

Then there's always the person who takes it just a little bit too far. Consider the video store owner who bought 1000 postcards from a cruise line. His headline read, "If your video store is full of ship, cruise on over to us." It did get a strong response, but in the process he offended a few customers. Be careful!

NEWSLETTERS

Communicating with your customers on a regular basis is important for a couple of reasons. First, you have to remind them that you're there. It's too easy for them to be seduced by competitors. Remember, it's much easier to keep a customer than to get a new one.

With a newsletter, you not only can provide that constant communication, but you provide it in a format that makes you appear to be the expert in your area. A newsletter, when done properly, lends a great deal of credibility to you. After all, you're not just selling goods and services, but also solutions to problems.

If you want to start a newsletter, here are some tips to help you along.

1. *Keep it simple*
Start with one page, 8 1/2 × 11, printed on two sides. If you don't have a computer, simply use a typewriter. There is no need to have the expense of typesetting.

2. *Have an artist create a masthead*
Even though you want to keep your production costs down, use a professionally designed masthead. Then your entire newsletter will look very professional, even when it's only done on a typewriter.
    You can actually preprint the letterhead in a couple of colors; then over-print the text as needed. That also helps keep your cost down while allowing you to have an attractive-looking piece.

3. *Use news items*
People don't want to read about the employee of the month or customer of the month. Put in information that they can use. And there's nothing wrong with giving prices of items in your newsletter, since that is information your customers need to know. You can even use it to preannounce sales. Give your preferred customers first choice of the sale merchandise.

4. *Start out on a quarterly or special-event basis*
Printing and distributing a newsletter every month may be too much for you at first.

5. *Keep your mailing list up-to-date*
Invite your customers to sign up for your mailing list. Mail it first class at least once every six months so you can get back those with old addresses that are no longer good.

6. *Put a coupon or free-drawing form in your newsletter from time to time to see how many people respond*

As with all of your promotional efforts, track results to see what works and what doesn't. With this valuable information, you can make them work better or drop them if they're just wasting money.

7. *Look to trade journals for interesting ideas for articles*
Quote your source. For example, "according to *U.S. Oil Week,* more consumers are getting their oil changed at quick oil change stores."

CROSS PROMOTIONS

Some of the cross promotions we talked about earlier fall into the "Postage without Paying" category. For example, when a Chamber of Commerce mailed a restaurant's 12-in-1 value card sheets to their members, there was a free mail campaign.

Even with the first cross promotion we talked about (Nautilus and Wildwood Raquet club), there was an insert in a mailing. To expand your customer base, consider stuffing your customer mailings with a partner's advertising, and they can do the same for you. You both win.

MARRIAGE MAILERS

Advo, ValPak, TriMark, and countless other services combine your coupon with others to provide an economical mailing. We've had some good responses from these types of mailings. Your results will obviously depend on your offer and the group that gets mailed.

The average cost seems to be about 5¢ per piece, although there have been some who have negotiated as low as 1 1/2¢ per piece. If they won't negotiate on price, perhaps you can get them to throw in a second color of ink at no charge or make yours the top piece.

Also insist on exclusivity. You want to be the only type of your business in the pack.

You may find that your results start to subside after three or four consecutive mailings. Track your results carefully. If you want to keep in the program to keep your competition out, you can reduce your offer or put no offer in at all—just promote your benefits.

DOOR HANGERS

An alternative to mailing in your community is to have a local nonprofit organization go door-to-door and distribute doorknob hangers. You might offer them 5¢ for each one they do, but a more powerful way is to provide them a bonus or commission based on redemption. Instead of a nickel for each one they pass out, offer them, for example, 50¢ for each one that comes back. This will make them work much harder, and you eliminate all of your risk.

Also, by converting this to a community-service program, be sure to put the name of the nonprofit group on the piece and announce that for each one redeemed, you'll donate to the cause.

If your local quick printer does not have the door knob die cut for your piece, they can just use a standard $1/4$ inch hole at the top and your nonprofit group can use a rubber band to attach your piece to the handle. The rubber band method works better even though it's just a little more complicated to get them to do it right.

The ideal size of your promotional piece is $1/3$ of a standard 8 $1/2 \times 11$ sheet of paper on card stock (67 pound). You'll get three pieces to the sheet, which helps keep your printing bill in check.

Door hangers can also be preprinted and on the shelf in case of an emergency. Let's say you have a blizzard and you know business is going to be dead for three or four days. With preprinted generic pieces ready to go, you can have them out that day. Obviously you can't have a sponsoring name on this particular piece, buy you can use a catchy generic headline such as "Disaster Deal: Because of the recent problem in our neighborhood, we're offering you something special."

The only other element you have to deal with is the expiration date. Instead of an actual date, put "offer expires 30 days from receipt of certificate." It works just fine and gives you unlimited shelf life for this particular piece.

SUMMARY

Both the telephone and the mail can be your most effective marketing tools—if you use them and use them properly. With the increased costs of postage and printing, you may want to explore using your phone more often as a promotional tool. After all, even in those cities in which you're paying for local calls, you only pay when you get an opportunity to present your message. With mail, on the other hand, you pay whether they read it or not.

Get your staff to start calling your customers to let them know of exciting things in your store. If you have a sale, call them. Offering a new product or service? Call them. Don't allow your salespeople to wait in the store for customers to come to them. Make them generate some foot traffic.

How to Squeeze More from Your Mass-Media Budget

The vast majority of our streetsmart marketing efforts are focused on the neighborhood level, yet mass-advertising media can be a very powerful tool to help you build sales. Obviously, you can't approach the local mass media in the same way that a chain or large franchise does, yet there are opportunities available to you.

You may be part of a big organization that provides you with media exposure on a national, regional, and even local level. That's great. Still, there are times you may want to take advantage of media opportunities to help your individual store.

The problem with using mass media, including TV, radio, print, and outdoor advertising is that you are paying based on the total size of the audience. A certain TV show, for example, may reach 100,000 people in your TV viewing area (often referred to as an Area of Dominate Influence or ADI). Those viewers may be watching from as far away as 10 to 15 miles, but the vast majority of your customers may come from a 3-mile radius of your store. Many of those 100,000 viewers, because of your location, would not even consider visiting your store. There is a great deal of waste.

Yet, with a limited budget and some streetsmarts, you can use these media very effectively.

In this chapter, we will look at a few different ways in which you can make the various advertising media work better for you in a single store and with a limited budget.

BILLBOARDS

Generally these are very expensive. For a single store, your best use of a billboard is as a directional. The board becomes an extension of your front sign and directs traffic to turn at a certain point so they'll know exactly how to get to your store. Use an arrow if it makes sense.

In designing your billboard, keep it very simple. Use one simple graphic and no more than six words in your message.

There are basically two types of billboards. The painted boards are the big ones. You often see them with graphics that extend past the board. That can produce an excellent impact, but these boards are the most expensive, and usually you're required to commit for a year.

The other board most commonly seen is referred to as a 30-sheet. These are the boards that use paper, and they're smaller than the painted boards. It's often hard to get a single board as a directional because the billboard companies like to sell them in multiples called "GRP Showings." The GRP stands for gross rating points, and they really have no tangible meaning for the average person. If they throw some terms like that at you, just nod and pretend that you understand, and they won't know the difference.

JUNIOR BILLBOARDS

There is an even smaller board called a Junior Board, which is more affordable and can be used as a directional as well. These boards require an even simpler message because they are so small.

THE BROAD SIDE

An economical alternative might be to get permission to paint your message on the side of a building at a strategic location. You might return the favor or negotiate a trade arrangement with the owner.

A well-placed bus bench or bus shelter might make a good directional for you, but on a limited budget, most of that type of advertising is too costly for what you get in return. If you think a bus advertisement might work for you, test it. There's a great deal of trial and error in business, especially in advertising. If it works for you, use it. If it doesn't, dump it.

FLEET EXPANSION

Speaking of transit advertising, don't overlook getting exposure from your own vehicles. The cost is minimal, and it works for you all of the time.

TRADING MARQUEES

If you have a marquee or a readerboard at your location, you can use it to communicate with passers-by. To get a different group of passers-by, trade one side of your board for a side of a board of another business on a different street. You can then both expand your exposure.

Many cities have ordinances banning the use of reader-boards, and some have very strict rules on signage. Be sure to investigate the ordinances in your local area.

There was a restaurant that was located off the main road, so if you didn't know it was there, you would drive right by. This was not good for business. The manager desperately wanted to put a portable readerboard at the edge of the parking lot near the road to let passers-by know the restaurant was there and ready to serve them.

Unfortunately, the city's elders passed an ordinance banning the use of these portable signs, but there was a grandfather clause in the law that allowed those who had them before the law was passed to keep them.

If there was some way to slip a sign in without anybody noticing, they might be able to keep it there for awhile. So the manager contacted the local Boy Scouts, who were looking for a place to sell Christmas trees for a fund raiser. He volunteered the front half of his parking lot to the organization and their worthy cause. To further help their cause, he provided a portable reader-board near the street to promote the Boy Scout Christmas tree sale.

He figured that no one in their right mind would keep the Boy Scouts from advertising their Christmas trees. He was right. The board stayed up from just before Thanksgiving through New Year's. After Christmas, the message was changed to thank everyone for their support of the Boy Scouts. After the first of the year, the message was changed to the luncheon special. As far as I know, it's still there today!

Basically, you should look for every opportunity to get as much free or low-cost outdoor exposure as you can. You would be surprised at the opportunities that can be found just by talking to people.

40 PERCENT SAVINGS

I once learned an interesting technique from a billboard sales-person. If you are planning to go with a showing of boards for a year, and if it is not critical that you have every single board up 100 percent of the time, he suggested that you buy every other month for a year. The savings would be about 40 percent, and you usually get a lot more than just your six months worth.

What happens is that they usually don't take the board down the exact day your month is up. Many of the boards will stay up extra days, weeks, or even all month. You'll probably get a great deal of extra exposure that you didn't pay for. You will have some extra production costs because the billboard company has to repaper the board every other month, but it should pay for itself.

This works great in winter, especially just after the first of the year when most retail advertisers take a hiatus. You might even rotate the locations of your boards to get more exposure.

NEGOTIATION POINTS

Billboard companies rarely negotiate price on their boards, especially with a small-dollar advertiser. Your point of negotiation is on location. Choose boards that are on high traffic areas with clear visibility. If you buy your board in the winter, check to see that there are no trees that will cover it up in spring and summer. See if the board is lighted and, if so, when the timer is set to go on and off.

One final word about outdoor advertising. It appears at this writing that its cost is only going to go up. There are more and more restrictions from communities that limit outdoor advertising on billboards and signs. As this happens, there will be less boards. Therefore, the ones remaining will be priced at a premium. You're going to have to be very creative about letting your customers know where you are.

RADIO ADVERTISING

Perhaps of all the local advertising media (with the possible exception of a very strategic directional billboard), radio advertising is the most affordable and effective local mass-advertising medium. But you can waste a fortune in it if you're not careful.

When my first book, *Streetfighting: Low Cost Advertising/ Promotions for Your Business* came out, I devoted a chapter to each of the mass media. The chapter on radio got me a lot of hate mail from radio stations. They particularly didn't like the techniques I used to negotiate a good buy from a radio salesperson. Since I started, just out of college, as a radio salesperson, I knew many of the tricks that were used to squeeze as much exposure for the dollar as possible.

I want to share with you some of the highlights of those pages, as well as some additional techniques. I've placed all of the mass-advertising media in one chapter because, for most of you reading this book, you'll have an advertising agency, either on a local or national level, handling most of it for you. Yet, there are often some good local opportunities for you to use outdoor, radio, TV, and print. You'll learn some of the critical essentials of dealing with the media salespeople.

These techniques might not work every single time, but some of them will work for you, and it will help you to get more for your money.

> *Radio Summit Meeting*—Most people negotiate a radio buy like they are negotiating for a used car. The radio salesperson comes to your business with a package of, for example, 50 commercials for $1000. You offer him $750. He hesitates and counters with $975. You flinch and counter back with $800. He plays with his portable calculator, frantically punching buttons, and fires back $850—it's the best he can do.

Why was your representative reluctant to negotiate with you? To understand, you have to see it from the representative's point of view. First of all, media representatives are usually paid a commission based on the gross amount of the sale. There is no direct cost of the service since they're selling air, but it does have a very limited shelf life. Once that minute is gone, it's gone forever. You can't pull it off a shelf and sell it at a later date. There are no day-old minutes available in radio.

For the sake of simplicity, let's say that your media representative is working on a 10 percent commission. When she comes to your store with a $1000 package of 50 30-second commercials, she's not thinking about $1000, but rather of the $100 commission she will have in her bank account if you sign the contract. Now, when you make a counter offer of $750, she's not thinking $750, but rather that she's losing $25. Then again, she doesn't want to blow the deal altogether, so she'll dicker with you to give up the absolute minimum to get the contract.

To turn this around, *set your budget up-front* from the time you begin talking to your representative about a radio schedule.

If you want to spend $850, you tell her that you have $850 to spend, then ask, "What can you do for me?" Be sure to ask for such information as the quote on 30-second spots, in "drive time," and so on.

Now she knows she'll make $85 if you sign the contract. She'll come to you with a proposal and perhaps offer you 40 spots. You flinch. (This is like having a mini heart attack. Pat your chest with an open hand and open your mouth in disbelief.) You insist that you need 65 spots for that money. She offers 45. You say no less than 60. She says she might be able to get you 50. You hold firm. Act as if you don't care all that much. If you get the 60 spots, you'll sign. If not, it's not worth it.

She's in a quandary. So, she goes back to the station and uses all of the sales training and experience she has to convince her sales manager why you have to get 40 percent more air time than most of the other advertisers. You've, in effect, turned their salesperson into your salesperson. She doesn't care, because she makes the same amount of commission regardless. She would even toss in the tower if it were up to her!

She comes back the next day to your store very excited. She got the approval. You smile and say, "Great. Toss in matching overnights, and it's final." She's come too far to give up now. Overnight spots are the ones that run from midnight to just before morning drive time—usually around 6:00 A.M. That's the most difficult part of the day for them to sell, since the audience is so small then. Often a station will toss in matching overnights for an additional 10 percent. So, in this case, you could get 60 more spots between midnight and 6:00 A.M. for a mere $85. But, unless you want that particular group, it's probably not worth paying for. On the other hand, if it's free, why not?

Have them do a five-second live-announcer tag. That's when the DJ comes in at the end of a commercial with a brief add-on announcement such as, "That's tomorrow night, so don't miss it." There's an important reason why I like these. First of all, it's live. There are so many commercials on radio that people have a tendency just to tune them out. Have you ever observed a teenager listen to the radio in a car? As soon as the song is over, they punch a button for more music. I doubt if most of them actually hear commercials.

These commercials are played in sequence during a commercial break. All things being equal, the most heard commercial in the sequence of six to eight would be the first and the last ones, since they're the closest to the music and the DJ's weather report.

When a DJ has a live tag to do, she usually waits until the last spot to do it because she has to come on again live anyway to give the traffic report, to give away a six pack of something to the ninth caller, and to introduce the next song. You have to provide your tag at the last possible minute so they don't have a chance to prerecord it.

When you give them your 5-second tag, give them about 8 to 9 seconds of copy, and be sure to use words that are difficult to pronounce. Tongue twisters are great.

Then listen in. As soon as the DJ starts speed reading through your live tag, they're certain to get tongue-tied and stumble over the words. This causes the audience to pay closer attention because it's unusual. Then the DJ will start joking about the mess up. I've heard them go on for as long as 10 minutes, joking about a flub to the guy in the helicopter giving the traffic situation. The point is that you get precious free minutes of air time that, because it's unusual, gets a great deal of attention and makes impact. Your message has a much greater chance of being remembered.

Here are a few more helpful hints on getting more impact from a local radio schedule on a very limited budget:

1. *Buy one station*

   Money talks. When you're negotiating your buy between two or three stations, let them know that it's a "one station buy." They'll work harder to get you more for your money because they're cutting their competition out as well. They like that.

2. *Never buy the "Number 1" station*

They're too arrogant. Since they are number one, they don't want to negotiate as much. From your point of view, however, it really doesn't matter if the station reaches 50,000 or 10,000. You have to be able to reach a given audience with *enough frequency* to make them take action. If one person hears your spot once or twice, it's a waste. They have to hear it three to five times or maybe more before you're going to make impact. If you advertise to a very large audience, you won't be able to afford enough frequency to make that impact. With a limited budget, frequency is more important than reach.

3. *Try to work with a station's newest salesperson*

They're the hungriest. A sales representative that has been there for 10 years has a good account list. Your little buy doesn't really matter to this person. But the new kid in town would kill for your business. He or she is starving and wants to prove to the boss that he or she can really do it.

If you haven't been assigned a sales representative, call the station and tell the receptionist, "I was talking to one of your sales representatives. I can't remember the name, but she just started not too long ago."

"Oh, you must mean Sandy Smith?"

"Sandy Smith. That's right. Could you have her give me a call?"

Ideally, you want the newest salesperson in the number three station.

4. *Concentrate your commercials*

Instead of spreading the 20 spots over a 1-week period, place them in a 3-day period. When you're on, get on strong. If you can't afford to be on strong, stay off until you can. You can also concentrate by the part of the day you are on the air—the day-part. Buy only Morning Drive or Mid-Day for one week. That way, you'll reach the same people over and over again, which is what you need in order to make impact.

5. *Radio remote broadcasts*
These packages can make some great impact for you. It creates excitement, usually gives a great amount of commercials the week prior to the event, and creates good impact. It can be a great traffic builder for you. Check them out. Listen for remotes and visit some to see how they work for other advertisers.

6. *Avoid station packages*
Usually when a station has a special package, it often benefits the station more than you. Be careful.

7. *Barter bummers*
Many stations will barter for air time. Trades are great for increasing your advertising dollars, but be careful. Make sure they give you the same cost per spot as they would when you pay cash for it. Stations have a tendency to want to use up your traded air time in not-so-good day-parts. Don't let them. If they want your product or service bad enough, you might be able to negotiate 2-for-1 or 3-for-1 trades. It really costs them no more out of their pocket, and if they want your business, they'll go for it.

8. *Give away "give-aways"*
This is a great way to get some additional free exposure. As a rule, they'll only provide an on-air give-away for paying advertisers; so when you're negotiating your buy, ask for it. It costs nothing to ask.

TELEVISION

For a single store, television is usually just too costly to work. If you belong to an advertising co-op group as part of your chain or franchise, and if you have a number of stores in the television viewing area, it does make sense. When you can afford to do TV right, it is the most powerful advertising medium. Yet, there are some little tricks you can do to take advantage of TV in your local market.

OPPORTUNITY PROGRAM BUYING

TV, like radio, is a frequency medium. Though frequency is a little less important on TV than on radio, it still takes a number of spots before someone will remember your message. However, there are some interesting opportunities in TV in which frequency isn't important enough to make impact. You bypass your need for frequency when your advertising message relates directly to the entertainment of the show.

There are many examples of this, but the most inexpensive is a talk show tie-in. Let's say that you own a hair salon, and that Phil Donahue brings a hair stylist who handles many Hollywood stars on his show as one of his guests. The TV audience is now focused on hair fashion. Just one or two commercials in that show with a simple message makes impact—far more than if your spot ran in another talk show that did not have such a guest.

Your sales representative can be very helpful in finding out who the guests are ahead of time. No matter what you sell, if you keep your eyes open and your ears to the ground, you'll often find some opportunities that will allow you to advertise on television and make impact.

With this approach, you can use 10-second spots, provided they're available. A 10-second spot costs half that of a 30, but you don't need a long message in this situation. Just let them know that you exist and where and how to find you, then tell them to call or visit. Ten seconds may be all you need. Also, you may want to buy one commercial in each of the commercial breaks of the show. It may take just three or four spots to dominate that show. It also keeps your competition from doing the same, since TV stations never put a direct competitor in the same commercial break.

One good idea is for a bookstore to use 10-second spot to promote a book that a mini-series or movie was made from. Travel agencies promote on *Love Boat* or *Hotel* reruns, and army surplus stores promote on *M*A*S*H*. The movie *Gran Prix* comes on, and so does the commercial for your quick oil change, auto painting, or parts store. When *Benji* hits the tube, so should your pet store spot. If you know that the FBI is releasing their crime statistics, your gun shop or karate school needs to pay whatever it takes to get a spot on the news.

Opportunity program buying ties into topical events such as the crime statistics mentioned above. If a child drowns, it is a good time to promote swimming lessons at the health club. If a major plant announces its closing, your truck or trailer rental needs to be on television.

National tie-in is another opportunity. If your company or supplier is running a big promotion on television, you can get a bigger piece of the pie with a smaller schedule of 10s letting the audience know where to buy it. For example, I remember working with a lawn and garden store that featured Toro lawn equipment.

Toro ran a huge TV campaign for four weeks in the market and rotated dealer tags, three to a spot. So, all of the Toro dealers got a small mention. To dominate this effort, our streetsmart Toro dealer ran a small schedule of 10s with the simple message, "your Toro headquarters," and the address and telephone number. Playing off the powerful exposure in the marketplace, he dominated the campaign on a shoestring budget.

INDEPENDENTS

In some markets you have a couple of independent stations. They may not have huge audiences, but they may be large enough to make it worth your while. Independents will negotiate better than network affiliates. Check out some late-night times. They are cheap, and with the proper frequency, they can make some impact for a store.

CABLE TV

There are many low-cost opportunities with your local cable company. They have spots available on networks, including M-TV, VH1, CNN, CNN Headline News, ESPN, and more. Make sure you're reaching the type of audience you want and that you get placed in good times. As of yet, these shows aren't covered by the rating services. Don't let the sales representatives make you think that they have huge audiences in your area. The number of households "hooked up" doesn't tell you how many people are seeing your commercial. This is worth some experimenting. Track your results. Negotiate as you learned to do with radio.

PBS

It might pay to look at a local sponsorship for a show that ties into your goods or services, such as "The Nightly Business Report" for a local bank or brokerage house; "This Old House" for any home center, hardware store, home improvements center, window replacements, and so on; cooking shows for restaurants or grocery stores; and painting shows for art schools or art supply stores. These sponsorships are low-key advertising, but they will provide you with a good target audience. Once you're a sponsor, do a cross promotion to get additional exposure when they have their telethon to raise money each year.

PRINT

The big thing that comes to mind when you think of print is newspaper. Unfortunately, there's not much you can do with your local daily newspaper. In most cities, there is only one newspaper in town—a monopoly. It's also very expensive. They don't negotiate price. A smaller advertiser almost has to beg to pay to get his or her ad in it. But if newspaper advertising works for you, then use it.

A few concepts to consider:

Full-page ad

If you're using a full-page ad and placement of that ad is not a factor, use the streetsmart cheater's full page. Drop that ad about four inches from the top and use one column less than full. This will save you about 20 percent with no appreciable loss of readership. If anything, the paper will place an editorial copy on the page and your readership will go up a little. However, if buying the full page guarantees that you're on the back page, this wouldn't make sense, since a back-page placement gets you additional readers.

Dominate ad

If you want to take the cheater's full page to the extreme, you can still dominate a page by keeping your ad about three inches above the centerfold and one more column wide than half. For example, your paper may be 22 inches tall by 9 columns wide. To dominate, run an ad that's 14 inches by 5 columns. No other ad can be larger than yours, and the cost is about 40 percent less than the full page. You can run an extra ad or buy some radio time with the money you have saved.

Small ads

Small ads in the paper can work for you if you keep your message simple and you have a strong benefit headline. I was working with a podiatrist who was very aggressive in his advertising. He ran some quarter-page ads in the local newspaper, but it just wasn't doing the job for him. He flew me in to fix it.

After reviewing the ads, I found the problem. He had hired a local advertising agency to do the ads. They were creating "cutsie" headlines like "Keep Your Best Foot Forward" or "Get Off on the Right Foot." They were cute, but they didn't sell.

After reading through the ads, I noticed that at the bottom, in very small print, was the invitation to "call for your free foot exam." I asked the doctor what this was, and he told me that he did, in fact, offer a free foot exam with no obligation. This allowed people to come in and see what the problem was, which usually resulted in setting up an appointment.

I cut the size of his ad by half, and in a big bold headline, I put "FREE FOOT EXAM." The ad also had his picture and some basic copy. We also put together a 30-second TV spot with the same concept and used the doctor as the talent on the spot.

It worked. He got immediate results from the ad, plus, since he was the talent in the spot and his picture was in the paper, he became a local celebrity. This worked particularly well in his office for establishing additional credibility with a patient. They saw him on TV and in the paper, and they more readily took his advice.

MAKE YOURSELF THE STAR

Regardless of the media you choose, it does help to make yourself the talent in your own advertising. Most advertising agency people hate doing this because it produces less exciting commercials and it is highly unlikely that it would be chosen for local ad awards. But when you make yourself a local celebrity, it helps you sell. You don't have to be tacky about it. There are many ways to do this tastefully. I've put a number of my clients on the air, in the paper, or on a billboard; when they were helping their customers, they sold more because of it.

PRINT ALTERNATIVES

There are local tabloids to consider. You may find that they have little pull, but you should test them. If possible, buy the front cover in two colors. For some reason, this seems to work.

Also look for your local business publication and perhaps a local magazine. Depending on your target audience, you could find an economical medium. Test and track. Don't expect them to have the same impact as your local daily newspaper, but they do cost much less. Look for a good return on your investment.

CO-OP ADVERTISING

Many venders and suppliers offer co-op advertising, in which you can get a big piece of your advertising reimbursed. Check it out. This can expand your ad budget, and you will be able to get it from places you never dreamed of.

Ask every one of your suppliers if they offer co-op advertising. Find out the rules and regulations. If they don't offer cash reimbursement for your advertising, they may provide additional products as compensation. Also ask about "key city money." This is where a vendor may stock pile unused co-op money and possibly make it available to you. You may get anywhere from 25 to 75 percent reimbursement, but there are programs that are 100 percent. It is a little extra paperwork on your part, but it's worth it.

While working with an appliance store, I discovered that they had a great deal of unused co-op money. White Westinghouse had a 75/25 program on their ranges and stoves. At the same time, the local gas company was running a co-op program that was 33 percent reimbursable on gas ranges and stoves. By coming up with a special campaign promoting White Westinghouse gas stoves, both vendors allowed the co-op on the same spots! This meant that on a $7000 buy, the appliance store received $7300 back in reimbursement, which was a $300 profit before they sold the first stove! They also moved a lot of stoves. Work with your vendors.

Converting Your Concepts to Combat

The best ideas in the world are useless unless you put them to work. As a result, most local store marketing programs fail in implementation. To take everything you learned in this book and make it work with all of your other locations, you need to have a good development and implementation plan of attack.

If you are the manager or operator of a single location, you need not read further. If you run or own more than one store, or supervise an ADI, region, district, or entire country, then this is the next critical phase. This chapter is designed to teach you how to develop and implement a system-wide streetfighting program on as large of a scale as you want.

Most companies put together a local store marketing manual complete with some fill-in-the-blank ad slicks that nobody uses. Other approaches include the "Chinese army" of marketing representatives going out into the field and setting up promotions for a number of stores. That won't work. Big companies want their ad agencies to provide them with local store marketing. It's unfair to ask your ad agency to do this. It's costly, and you're asking them to do things that are not their forte. It won't work.

The only way to get a local store marketing program to work is by having it executed on the store level by (or supervised by) store manager. Pure and simple. Any other approach does not work. If you're not willing to let your manager or their assistants do this, then you're wasting your time.

In order to get the cooperation of your store managers, you must have capable area supervisors who can guide the managers in their efforts. Then the supervisors' supervisors need to know as well—all the way up to the VP of marketing and operations, if need be.

The point is that this program is a "bottoms-up" program. It's developed at the store level by store level management. It's executed on the store level by store level management. All the levels of management above the store level guide and supervise, but they do not do the actual work of planning, developing, or implementing.

Also, this is the only marketing program that works best when executed out of the operations department as opposed to the marketing department. Marketing works best separate from the store level, but operations, on the other hand, deals on a regular basis with the store level management. Marketing and operations are usually at odds, but in this case they're not, because marketing merely advises the operations side.

Execution by store level management and supervised by operations are two ideas that, no doubt, are a major departure from the way most companies work. Yet, this is how your local marketing program will get you results. Any other approach will fail.

YOUR GOAL

The 12-month development phase of your program serves a number of purposes: (1) By the end of 12 months, you have a neighborhood marketing program that is effective and proven in the field. (2) you have a "Train-the-Trainers" program for your supervisors that is also proven. (3) You have a group of stores, managers, and supervisors who serve as a role-model to the rest of the organization. It proves to them that it does work and applies subtle peer pressure for them to make it work. (4) You have a prototype market(s) where you can test crazier promotions and newer ideas without jeopardizing the growth of the standard local store marketing program throughout the organization.

Rolling out without this 12 months of testing, development, improving, adapting, and modifying kills your program. That means that if upper management is serious about making such a program work, they have to have the patience to allow the development phase to work properly. I've seen perfectly good programs fail because there was not enough time given to the development. Then the entire system started doing programs that weren't fully developed and field tested. The result was numerous frustrated managers who sabotaged the program. It was dropped. If you're going to do it, do it right.

Sometimes upper management seems to look at this type of program as the answer to their prayers. It is, however, not a magic act. You have to have a successful company to begin with and be producing good products and good service before a local marketing program can work. This is not a replacement or cure-all for a company in trouble, but rather an enhancement to a successful operation that wants to get a major edge over their competition. In all likelihood, depending upon the size and make-up of your organization, count on a two- to three-year period from the beginning to the time when all of your stores are using it.

Time Commitment: Store Level

Once up and running, your store manager need only spend a few hours a week in 5 to 15 minute increments on his or her local store marketing efforts. It's not a full-time job, but it is a full-time commitment, just as there is a full-time commitment to keeping the store clean, providing fast service, providing products of high quality, and making sure your employees are pleasant. You must also make this effort in local store marketing; it's integrated into your business.

Your manager has a checklist. She has to hire new employees, make sure the restroom is clean, schedule vacations, cash out the register, and do her two promotions for the week. It's that simple.

To be effective, you'll develop your local store marketing program working with a few developmental markets and anywhere from 15 to 50 managers. The in-field development lasts between 9 and 18 months, but 12 months seems ideal since you want to make sure you've covered all the seasons and special promotions. Don't go less than 9 months. It's just not enough time to work out all the bugs, including techniques for getting store managers to do this on an on-going basis.

The following is a brief outline on the stages of the 12-month development of your local marketing program. Each of these elements will be explained in step-by-step detail later in this chapter.

MONTH 1

Your first month is spent preparing for your initial seminar, which will be presented to all the participating store managers and their supervisors to kick off your program. Before you can do this, you must do the following:

1. Develop your own initial streetfighting neighborhood marketing seminar, which will be geared for your business.

   a. Collect all written and recorded neighborhood marketing techniques that are applicable.

    b. Survey your own managers for their successes and ideas.

    c. Conduct your own neighborhood marketing program for a month with one store.

2. Prepare a detailed outline for a full-day training seminar.

    a. Include role-playing and exercises.

    b. Add interesting stories.

3. Develop a support seminar workbook with ad slicks.

    a. The fill-in-the-blank portion becomes their customized neighborhood marketing plan of attack.

    b. Ad slicks are approved and ready for store's address.

4. Select your developmental markets and participating managers.

    a. Have at least five stores per market.

    b. Use middle to high-volume stores only.

MONTH 2

1. Conduct your full-day seminar.

    a. Include all participating managers.

    b. Invite participating supervisors.

    c. Include appropriate corporate marketing and operations people.

2. Immediately following the seminar, train managers one-on-one.

    a. 2–3 Promotions per week

      1) Merchant certificates

    2) Value cards

    3) Community involvement

    4) Internal programs

    5) Major promotions

3. Follow up one-on-one training with written reinforcement. Send copies to supervisors, corporate headquarters, and your own file.

4. Starting the following week, conduct your weekly telephone follow-up training and consulting with each participant:

    a. By appointment, once a week for three weeks

    b. Work from agenda

5. Follow up the phone consultation/training session with written reinforcement.

6. Write monthly status report.

MONTH 3

1. At the beginning of each month, in each market, conduct a half-day workshop to:

    a. Review past month's activities

    b. Set goals for next month

    c. Trouble-shoot

    d. Work on new ideas and techniques

    e. Group sharing of successes and ideas

    f. Work from agenda

2. Follow up with review memo.

3. Continue weekly telephone training and consulting with each participant.

4. Have a written follow up after each phone consultation/training session including:

   a. Informal note

   b. Copy to supervisor

MONTH 4

1. Repeat Month 3.

   a. Continue to trouble-shoot and improve offers and techniques.

   b. Keep managers excited and motivated.

   c. Document results and failures.

   d. Work on program variety and variations.

2. Begin working with supervisors on training the trainers.

3. Supervisors set up promotions on a multi-store basis.

4. Managers drop back to one promotion a week.

5. Managers start community involvement biggie promotion.

MONTHS 5–12

1. Continue as before. Improve, modify, and document.

   a. Monthly group workshop

   b. Workshop memo

   c. Weekly telephone consulting/training

   d. Follow-up note

The goal is that at the end of 12 months, you will have a tried-and-true local store marketing program complete with 15 to 50 corporate local store heroes and some very good "war stories." Launching the program without going through this developmental stage invites disaster because you have managers doing a program that hasn't had the bugs worked out. If you're going to have success with this, make sure you know what works and what doesn't before the roll-out.

At the same time you're developing your local store marketing program for your store managers, you're also working on the supervisor's program. The people that supervise the store managers not only need to be able to do the program for themselves, but have to be able to guide their managers to do it for themselves. They need both sets of skills.

While you're working with your local store managers, you are also working with the supervisors on your "StreetSmart Train-the-Trainers" program. Your supervisors might be called area supervisors, field marketing representatives, field operations representatives, or franchise support. The name isn't important, but working with those people in your organization who work with the store managers on a regular basis is important.

The best time to bring the supervisors into this phase of the program is about four months in, after you have your store managers up and running. Remember, you're building from the ground up.

That doesn't mean that your supervisors are standing by idle. During those first three months, it's their job to set up promotions for the store on a multi-store basis. For example, the minit-lube/Dairy Queen two-way cross promotion (Figure 2-13) is the type of program that a supervisor would instigate.

A supervisor cross promotion might just be a program where three of your stores and three stores in another chain work together. The point is, get your supervisors involved.

Now we'll examine the elements of the first four months in greater detail.

CUSTOMIZING YOUR LOCAL STORE MARKETING PRESENTATION

You want to make it as easy as possible for your test managers to use this program, so you need to prepare as much as possible. Obviously, this program will be far less customized and effective than the one you'll present after 12 months of development, but you have to start somewhere.

RESEARCH

You need to learn as much about local marketing as possible, as well as important skills in management, time management, selling, communications, customer service, and so on. In the appendix of this book you'll find a list of books, audio cassette albums, videotapes, and other resources that have been very helpful in the development of the actual neighborhood marketing program we teach. It also covers the necessary skills required for training managers and implementing a system-wide program successfully.

Your goal is to develop a program that is designed specifically for your company. Instead of using examples that I have used in this book, use your own company's stories complete with your own corporate local-store heroes. Tom Peters in *In Search of Excellence* talks about the importance of creating your own corporate folk heroes who reinforce the corporate goals. To get your local marketing program up and running, you need the same.

FIELD SURVEY

One other very important source of local store material for you is within your own company. Although you could do it through the mail, the most effective way to gather up your company's neighborhood marketing success stories is with a telephone survey.

First survey the supervisors to find out the store managers who have been very aggressive in their marketing efforts.

Once you get a list of streetfighting store managers, call them up and interview them. Find out what kind of programs that they did that really worked for them. Get numbers, such as how many redemptions, new customers, the cost of the program, the return on investment, how much increase in sales, and anything else that helps to paint a picture for your soon-to-be streetsmart managers.

You really need to probe to find out what they did and how they did it. Get all the details, because you not only want to share the idea or technique, but also all of the colorful stories that make sharing the idea more meaningful and interesting. Remember, to be an effective trainer, you have to have a little bit of flair for the theatrical. After all, what good are all of your great ideas if you can't get your managers to remember them or be motivated to use them.

Also, if the promotion they did involves a printed piece like a certificate or flier, have them send it to you. It will look good in your workbook and will help build credibility for your program.

Put It All Together

Design your seminar so that it not only informs the participants of the various types of promotions that are available, but also so that they can practice their approach. For example, when you teach how to set up a cross promotion, your workbook should have a copy of a sample script. Once you go through how to do it, pair your group up and practice setting them up. Role playing is an effective way to get the group's involvement.

Lecturing to them will not get results. Involve your group in the program. Make them do it for themselves. It's only after they have done this repeatedly that it becomes easier for them to do.

Most people who participate in such a program are literally scared to death of anything that remotely looks like sales. Asking another merchant to hand out your advertising for you is a sale, and it scares a manager to death. Yet, when they realize how easy it is and how fun it can be, they soon forget their fears. This portion of your seminar should be fun and effective.

Work from a detailed outline rather than from a script. Use slides or overheads to stress key points. Leave nothing to chance with these people. Also, it works best if after each key point, you illustrate it with a story. Stories are good to help your managers remember what you're teaching them. Keep in mind that you're not up there doing a "stand-up" routine. Each story, quote, anecdote, illustration, and even joke is there to reinforce a point.

I was in Toronto to deliver a half-day seminar sponsored by Pepsi for their Pizza Hut and Taco Bell managers and area supervisors. I arrived the night before at the resort where their conference was being held, and I found that many of my participants were up very late partying. They would undoubtedly be very tired the next morning at 9:00 A.M. when I was scheduled to begin.

Sure enough, the next morning my participants didn't look very motivated. It was going to be a real challenge to keep them from nodding off during my presentation. I had to act fast.

My opening remarks were a few humorous notes about the party the night before and how a party like that is a presenter's worst nightmare. So I let them know that there would be no sleeping in my program. I then offered to the first participant who caught another participant nodding off a free copy of my book, *Streetfighting,* if they would get up, go over to the participant, lightly tap them on the head and yell "Got Ya!"

That got some laughs. It also kept a lot of people attentive. About half an hour into the program, one young manager in the middle of the group stood up and walked over to the other side of the room to a woman in the third row. He tapped her on the head and yelled, "Got Ya!"

Everyone laughed. The woman protested, however, saying that she was merely glancing down to review her notes. I gave them both a book for helping to keep the rest of the group awake.

This little game is just one example of a way to have fun in your program. You don't want to be obnoxious about it, but you do want to get people motivated to learn. As circumstances dictate, you'll come up with your own ways to stress points or solve certain problems. You'll want to incorporate those that work into your presentations and drop those that don't work.

Just like your streetfighting program, your presentation skills and ability to train people also improves with experience. Don't be afraid to experiment. Also, I like to record my presentations so I can review how I did. Although it's just an amateur recording, it's enough to let me see for myself areas that need improving in order to give a more effective presentation.

To start putting your seminar together, you may want to start with the rough outline below. These are some of the main sections and subheads we use when presenting our streetfighting program. From this, modify and adapt it to your needs, then with the headings left, expand into greater detail. When you're done, you will be able to deliver your entire presentation from about a five page, single-spaced outline:

1. Introduction to neighborhood marketing concept
   a. Carving off your territory and protecting it
   b. Primary service area where you get 90 percent of your business
   c. Why we need local store marketing
   d. How it gives us a jump over our competition
2. Retail merchant certificates
   a. How a cross promotion works
   b. The 3-Cs of cross promotions

3. How to set up (sell) the cross promotion

   a. Presenting the "you" benefits

   b. 10 Steps in setting up a cross promotion

   c. Stories of successful cross promotions

   d. Tracking results and why it's important

4. Cross promotion variations

   a. Value card

   b. 2-Way vs. 1-way

   c. 12-in-1

   d. Ticket-to-event

   e. Reverse

5. Community service

   a. The "donation dollar" program

   b. The annual "biggie" program

   c. The event related "biggie"

   d. High visibility/low liability concept

   e. Turning a promotion into a community service

   f. Publicity possibilities

   g. Turning down donation requests

6. Internal marketing

   a. Up-sell contest for employees

   b. Referral contests for employees

   c. Referral contests for customers

   d. Point-of-sale programs

7. Special events

    a. Grand opening

    b. Competitive intrusion

    c. Blow out

    d. Disaster promotion

8. Mass media overview

    a. Radio promotions

    b. Outdoor

    c. Others when applicable

9. Direct mail and tele-selling

    a. Getting customer lists

    b. When to mail and when to call

    c. How to set appointments

    d. How to answer phones

    e. Getting free inserts

10. Getting started

    a. 10 Steps for getting started

    b. Setting priorities

    c. Short-range vs. long-range goals

    d. Setting up company-wide networking of participants

Each of these sections can be expanded in much greater detail, but it's up to you to pick and choose which sections make sense for you as well as how much detail you need in any one of them.

Your goal is not to overwhelm your participants, but rather to expose them to all of the possibilities they have in their neighborhoods, to train them so they're comfortable and effective in networking in their neighborhoods, then to give them their first (idiot-proof) assignment to set up when they get back to their store.

Even though you are customizing this seminar for your developmental participants, you're mostly working with generic and unproven ideas—unproven, that is, in your particular organization. That makes the developmental phase of your overall program the most difficult and the most critical.

To get your pilot program off the ground, you'll have to pull out all the stops. You'll use every possible training and communications approach you can. After the seminar is complete, your managers and supervisors will be at the highest level of enthusiasm that they're ever going to be at. Don't let this go to waste. The seminar, by itself, is not enough to make this work.

SEMINAR WORKBOOK

To go along with your seminar, each of your attendees should have a workbook to serve primarily as the local marketing plan for the manager's store. Put exercises in the workbook in which the manager thinks about his or her location and writes down 10 retail merchants in his or her neighborhood who would make good cross-promotion partners. Then have them look at those 10 names and see how many decision makers in those organizations are their customers. That way, they already know the first 3 or 4 people to contact, and they can do it without leaving the store.

Have the same type of exercise for value cards, community services, and so on. In all, there are over 100 potential cross promotions to go after, all in priority, so when the managers get back to their stores, they can immediately set up their first three promotions with no trouble.

Your workbook contains transcripts of what to say and how to say it. Key points are fill-in-the-blank. Remember to involve them. Have some samples of cross-promotion pieces that they can use for practice and setting up their first promotions.

In the back are your cross-promotion shells—ad slicks with all of the artwork done. All your people need to do is to put in the store's address and phone and they're ready to go. All copies and disclaimers are already approved by the corporation, so they don't have to ask permission when they want to do a promotion. The actual printing is done at their neighborhood quick printer, but since the artwork is already approved, there's very little chance of a mistake.

Suggested ad slicks are printed on $8\frac{1}{2} \times 11$ coated stock and include the following versions:

1) Merchant certificate   2-up
2) Merchant certificate   4-up (used for large volume promos)
3) Value-card   3-up
4) Employee incentive contest   4-up (horizontal format)
5) Donation dollar   6-up

Other types of ad slicks include:

6) Donation dollar flier   1-up
7) 12-In-1 Value card   (this was shown in Chapter 2)
8) Gift certificates
9) Free cards
(Several of these are illustrated in Figures 9-1 to 9-5.)

If you want to provide a few different types of offers, you'll need additional slicks for each offer and in each appropriate format. For example, if you have two merchant certificate offers, like save $2 and another for save $3, you would provide the two different versions for both the 2-up and 4-up slicks. Make this as easy as possible for your managers to complete their promotions. If the printer has to change something, it causes delays, diminished motivation, and eventually failure.

Figure 9-1   Merchant certificate ad slick, 2-up.

Figure 9-2   Merchant certificate ad slick, 4-up.

Dear Employee:

Recently, we arranged with Great Clips located at:

for you to get your own Special Free 60 Day Value Card.

With your Free Value Card, you'll be able to receive a 10% savings on all Great Clips Services and Products. Simply detach your Value Card below and show it the next time and every time you visit Great Clips.

Your Free Value Card can be used over and over for as long as indicated by the expiration date below. Please note that this special arrangement is not valid in combination with any other offer and is subject to the terms and conditions stated on your card.

Your Free Value Card is provided specifically for your use only. Great Clips reserves the right to ask for identification to verify your affiliation with us.

We're very pleased to provide you this extra benefit so feel free to start using it right way.

Great Clips
Nobody does you like we do.

FREE VALUE CARD

the bearer of this card is affiliated with

((insert name of xpr partner))

and is entitled to a 10% savings on Great Clips Services and Products. Not valid with any other offer. Valid only at:
Expires:

Dear Employee:

Recently, we arranged with Great Clips located at:

for you to get your own Special Free 60 Day Value Card.

With your Free Value Card, you'll be able to receive a 10% savings on all Great Clips Services and Products. Simply detach your Value Card below and show it the next time and every time you visit Great Clips.

Your Free Value Card can be used over and over for as long as indicated by the expiration date below. Please note that this special arrangement is not valid in combination with any other offer and is subject to the terms and conditions stated on your card.

Your Free Value Card is provided specifically for your use only. Great Clips reserves the right to ask for identification to verify your affiliation with us.

We're very pleased to provide you this extra benefit so feel free to start using it right way.

Great Clips
Nobody does you like we do.

FREE VALUE CARD

the bearer of this card is affiliated with

((insert name of xpr partner))

and is entitled to a 10% savings on Great Clips Services and Products. Not valid with any other offer. Valid only at:
Expires:

Dear Employee:

Recently, we arranged with Great Clips located at:

for you to get your own Special Free 60 Day Value Card.

With your Free Value Card, you'll be able to receive a 10% savings on all Great Clips Services and Products. Simply detach your Value Card below and show it the next time and every time you visit Great Clips.

Your Free Value Card can be used over and over for as long as indicated by the expiration date below. Please note that this special arrangement is not valid in combination with any other offer and is subject to the terms and conditions stated on your card.

Your Free Value Card is provided specifically for your use only. Great Clips reserves the right to ask for identification to verify your affiliation with us.

We're very pleased to provide you this extra benefit so feel free to start using it right way.

Great Clips
Nobody does you like we do.

FREE VALUE CARD

the bearer of this card is affiliated with

((insert name of xpr partner))

and is entitled to a 10% savings on Great Clips Services and Products. Not valid with any other offer. Valid only at:
Expires:

Figure 9-3 Value card, 3-up.

Great Clips® Now You Have A Friend at Great Clips!

SAVE $2 to $10

Just because your friend is a valued employee at Great Clips you can now save $2 on the regular price of a hair cut or $10 on the regular price of a perm. Isn't it great to have friends in important places!

Not valid with any other offer. Only one special employee value per person. Valid only at the following Great Clips locations:

_____
(insert address, locater, phone)

Authorized by _____   Expires: _____

Nobody does you like we do.®

Great Clips® Now You Have A Friend at Great Clips!

SAVE $2 to $10

Just because your friend is a valued employee at Great Clips you can now save $2 on the regular price of a hair cut or $10 on the regular price of a perm. Isn't it great to have friends in important places!

Not valid with any other offer. Only one special employee value per person. Valid only at the following Great Clips locations:

_____
(insert address, locater, phone)

Authorized by _____   Expires: _____

Nobody does you like we do.®

Great Clips® Now You Have A Friend at Great Clips!

SAVE $2 to $10

Just because your friend is a valued employee at Great Clips you can now save $2 on the regular price of a hair cut or $10 on the regular price of a perm. Isn't it great to have friends in important places!

Not valid with any other offer. Only one special employee value per person. Valid only at the following Great Clips locations:

_____
(insert address, locater, phone)

Authorized by _____   Expires: _____

Nobody does you like we do.®

Great Clips® Now You Have A Friend at Great Clips!

SAVE $2 to $10

Just because your friend is a valued employee at Great Clips you can now save $2 on the regular price of a hair cut or $10 on the regular price of a perm. Isn't it great to have friends in important places!

Not valid with any other offer. Only one special employee value per person. Valid only at the following Great Clips locations:

_____
(insert address, locater, phone)

Authorized by _____   Expires: _____

Nobody does you like we do.®

Figure 9-4   Employee Incentive contest cards, 4-up.

Choosing Your Managers and Markets

This is not a test. That's why we refer to our chosen markets as developmental markets, not test markets. In choosing both markets and managers, you need to look for a number of things.

First, work only with middle to high volume stores that are run by sharp managers. There will be pressure from certain persons to take on the losing stores and make them successful. This phase *is not a turn-around program.* However, once the development phase is finished, you can work on special applications such as turn arounds of low volume stores, competitive intrusions, grand openings, change of managers, and so on.

The purpose of your development phase is to take the basic ideas presented in this book, along with all of the other local marketing ideas and information you find, and mold them specifically to your organization's needs. The higher volume stores help you do this better and faster. Once you develop a program that gets results, it's much easier to apply it to a turn-around situation.

Secondly, make sure you have enough participating managers to make the program work. Having too few managers won't provide you with enough promotions to build momentum or to try different offers, formats, partners, and so on. By the same token, too many managers slow down the entire process. Depending on the size of your organization, I would suggest a minimum of 15 managers, but no more than 50. Allow for management turn over if you traditionally lose 30 percent of your managers in a 12-month period, you had better start with 20 to end up with 15.

Third, choose markets in which the managers are "clustered." You need to work them; they can also feed off of each other. Try to choose markets in which you have at least five participating stores in the same basic area. If you can have more than five, it's even better. You also want at least two markets. I would suggest no more than four or five markets.

Great Clips

Nobody does you like we do.

GREAT BUCK

Redeemable only at the locations listed on the back.

Not valid with any other offer.

Your local Great Clips supports a wide variety of community projects. We may be able to help with your next fund-raising drive. Contact your local Great Clips manager for further details.

GREAT BUCK FOR YOU AND OUR COMMUNITY!

Great Clips

Nobody does you like we do.

GREAT BUCK

Redeemable only at the locations listed on the back.

Not valid with any other offer.

Your local Great Clips supports a wide variety of community projects. We may be able to help with your next fund-raising drive. Contact your local Great Clips manager for further details.

GREAT BUCK FOR YOU AND OUR COMMUNITY!

Great Clips

Nobody does you like we do.

GREAT BUCK

Redeemable only at the locations listed on the back.

Not valid with any other offer.

Your local Great Clips supports a wide variety of community projects. We may be able to help with your next fund-raising drive. Contact your local Great Clips manager for further details.

GREAT BUCK FOR YOU AND OUR COMMUNITY!

Great Clips

Nobody does you like we do.

GREAT BUCK

Redeemable only at the locations listed on the back.

Not valid with any other offer.

Your local Great Clips supports a wide variety of community projects. We may be able to help with your next fund-raising drive. Contact your local Great Clips manager for further details.

GREAT BUCK FOR YOU AND OUR COMMUNITY!

Great Clips

Nobody does you like we do.

GREAT BUCK

Redeemable only at the locations listed on the back.

Not valid with any other offer.

Your local Great Clips supports a wide variety of community projects. We may be able to help with your next fund-raising drive. Contact your local Great Clips manager for further details.

GREAT BUCK FOR YOU AND OUR COMMUNITY!

Great Clips

Nobody does you like we do.

GREAT BUCK

Redeemable only at the locations listed on the back.

Not valid with any other offer.

Your local Great Clips supports a wide variety of community projects. We may be able to help with your next fund-raising drive. Contact your local Great Clips manager for further details.

GREAT BUCK FOR YOU AND OUR COMMUNITY!

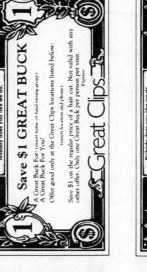

Figure 9-5 Donation dollar, 6-up (Front and Back).

207

Another consideration is the participation and cooperation you'll get from the supervisors of the participating stores. Remember, you not only develop the managers' program, but you also develop the supervisors' program by the end of your 12-month period.

ONE-ON-ONE TRAINING

Immediately after the seminar, start working with the managers one-on-one. This is very time consuming, and it will be a tough couple of weeks for you, but you have to make sure that they get their first few promotions set up within the first week or two after the seminar. Go with them. Set up the first one for them so they see how it is done. Watch them set up the next one. Take them by the hand if need be, but don't leave until they are set.

You should be able to handle four to five stores in one day in the field, provided the five stores are in a reasonable driving distance from each other. You only need 90 minutes at any location. Don't spend the entire day with them. When you visit the store, set up that portion of the seminar exercises that lists 10 potential cross-promotion partners, then check off the ones who are already your customers.

The first or second cross promotion you set up with them need not be with the best type of partner. All you want to do at this stage is to build the manager's confidence that he or she can handle anything.

WRITTEN REINFORCEMENT

After every contact you make, whether it is in a group, one-on-one, or over the telephone, always follow-up with something in writing. There are no hard-core rules of how you should provide this written follow-up. This helps your managers remember what you discussed and keeps up that subtle pressure for them to do this program.

After phone calls, I usually use a handwritten or typed memo. It's very informal. After the monthly group workshops, I issue a memo similar to the minutes from a meeting. This is a little more formal and goes to a number of different people (Figure 9-6).

At least on a quarterly basis, you need to do a status report. This report contains not only a review of what has been done, but also your plans for the near future (Figure 9-7).

These written follow-ups provide you with a number of things. First, they reinforce to your managers everything you worked on. After a verbal session, they get something in writing. This keeps up the pressure. Secondly, copies of all of these notes, memos, and reports go into your files. When you talk with your managers every week, you have a record of what you discussed the week before. You know what they've been working on. I actually take notes on the photocopy of the last week's notes. From that I write my new notes.

Another advantage of this written follow-up is that you can send confidential copies to the manager's supervisor. This keeps supervisors informed as to what their managers are up to. Also, when you start your "Train-the-Trainers" program, your supervisors see how you work, and it makes it easier for you to gradually transfer some of those training responsibilities.

PHONE CONSULTATION AND TRAINING

One of the keys to your success in the program is having *weekly* verbal contact with your participating managers. To do this in person is very time consuming and practically impossible. Yet, with the use of the phone, you can make the same impact as a weekly one-on-one training session.

The phone is becoming our most effective tool in development and training. You have a limited amount of time, and by integrating the proper use of the phone in your training efforts, you can accomplish five times as much without spending more time or losing effectiveness.

Streetfighter

Marc E. Slutsky

NAME: Bob _____ DATE: 3/12/87

WEEK OF: 3/12/87-3/19/87

GOALS: Butcher Shop (500)

1. Stitches and Such (1000)
2.
3.
4.

NEXT WEEK:

1. To set up two more Cross Promotions by next week.
2.
3.
4.

Date of next phone call: 3/19/87 at 11:00 A.M. your time.

Comments:

The two Cross Promotions you have set up have the distribution we like. At least 500. I know it takes a lot of time to set up Cross Promotions. At least in the beginning. But it will all be worth it in the future. Keep up the good work and I will talk to you next week.

Retail Marketing Institute
1122 NORTH ALMA ROAD, SUITE 216 B, RICHARDSON, TEXAS 75081 (214) 231-9105

Streetfighter

Memo from

Marc Slutsky
Vice President

5/1/87

Bob,

Congratulations on the response you got with the American Fasion Institute. I think that is great you sold one 990 and two Sergers off that Cross Promotion.

Keep me posted on what you are doing with all the information you received from the questionaires. We need to take advantage of this opportunity.

Remember our goals for the month is to have one type of promotion each week for a total of four. Looking forward to your phone call on Friday the 8th of May at 11:15 A.M. your time.

Take care,

Retail Marketing Institute
1122 N Alma Road   Suite 216 B
Richardson, TX 75081
214/231-9105

Figure 9-6 (Left) Typewritten memos and (Right) follow up letters provide feedback to customers.

Streetfighter®

Retail Marketing Institute
34 W. Whittier Street   Columbus, Ohio 43206
614/443-5555

Viking Streetfighting Memo

Date: 4/1/87
To: Streetfighting Viking Dealers
From: Marc Slutsky
Re: April 1st Meeting Review
cc: Jeff, Brent, Stan, John

A very interesting and exciting meeting! First we reviewed the past month's activities. Good stuff happening all around. Everyone has set up some Cross-Promotions. Nat's Mark Pi promotion taught us a very important lesson: Always try to set up promotions with people that speak English! Bob had four set up, Kathy has four in the works, and Mike's bank stuffer just went out.

The Viking Buck was reviewed and an idea for a fund raiser discussed. Offer a charity group a certain amount of money (perhaps $1) for each person that comes in for 990 Discovery. You could use an variation of a Cross-Promotion piece but instead of an offer to the user, the reward goes to the charity group. Would work great for Mike who want to reach more Menonites as a target group.

Kathy will work a Viking Buck promotion with the American Red Cross program where she has donated a quilt for a raffle. They're also having a bake sale and a cook book sale where the Viking Bucks might make a great tie in and perhaps on a city-wide basis.

A blue print was laid out for the following 16 weeks whereby each dealer will get at least one promotion each week. These promotions will vary but by the time we reach the first of August, each dealer will have completed about 20 promotions in all. They will include Merchant Cross-Promotions, Value Cards, Customer Referral, Viking Bucks, Fund Raiser, Ticket To Event, and some others. A Viking Streetfighting Chart Of Promotions was handed out to illustrate the variety of promotions.

Each Dealer signed a "Streetfighting Agreement", making their total commitment to the program including making phone calls, setting up promotions, working with others in the group, etc.

Consistency is the key to success. Get the promotions set up, carried out, delivered, and forgotten. Then go to the next one. Once we master the basics, next month we'll go over more advanced techniques.

Stan will provide line art for the Ultra Suede Cosmetic Bag and Sew Chest. We'll update artwork when that is completed. Everyone received the second round of art slicks. Kathy provided everyone with the Cosmetic Bag Pattern. Much excitement over this offer.

Next meeting is Thursday, April 30th. Starts 9:00 AM SHARP. Be there. Bring your workbooks and samples of your promotions (enough for everyone). It's important that everyone be there, so please plan around it.

Figure 9-7   Status report to keep everyone informed.

The phone alone isn't enough, but as a weekly supplement to your monthly group meetings, it is a perfect way to keep in touch, keep your managers on target, and troubleshoot problems before you lose an entire month.

While on the phone trying to get a manager to modify a promotion in order to get more out of it, don't tell them what to do. Rather, ask questions and get them to figure it out for themselves. Your job is not to prove to everybody how good you are at this. You're much more valuable to the company if you can get the managers to do it. You serve more as a coach. Even after you talk about a successful program, you might ask the question, "As successful as this promotion was, what would you do differently to make it even better next time?" Build on success.

It's also important that you remember that this is not their only responsibility at the store. As a matter of fact, it's probably one of the least important priorities in their mind. If an employee calls in sick, a supplier can't make a delivery, the power goes out, and the toilet in the men's room is overflowing, promotions are the least of their concerns. At the same time, you have to know whether they're really dealing with emergencies or just creating emergencies to avoid doing what they need to do.

It takes constant but subtle pressure to get managers to do their programs. You don't need a lot in a short period of time, but rather a few each week over a long period of time. You have to be able to incorporate these activities in with all the other responsibilities that they have.

To check yourself to see just how effective you are on the phone, record some of your telephone consultations and play them back for your review. Listen to yourself and see how effective you were in helping your managers and supervisors get on track. Remember, this is just for your personal review. Nobody else is going to hear it.

Guiding your neighborhood level managers in your own Streetfighter marketing program is a very big challenge and you'll need all of the help you can get. Recently we have enhanced the productivity of our field training staff by computerizing their telephone activities.

We were able to do this with the help of one particular telemarketing software program called *TeleMagic* developed by the Remote Control Computer Support Group, Inc.

We first started using this software for our telephone salesforce and it performed wonderfully but more importantly it was obvious to us that our tele-consulting efforts and our tele-selling efforts were very much the same kind of activity only "selling" a different idea to different people.

Because our field-training force travels so much, we use laptop computers. TeleMagic is designed for IBM compatible machines using MS Dos. You need at least 512K of RAM but the developers suggest 620K of RAM. It can be run with two floppies but we suggest you get a 20 meg hard drive. The TeleMagic software package comes with both the 5 1/4-inch floppies for a standard desktop machine and also on 3 1/2-inch diskette for the laptop which you can download right into your hard drive. You may also want to get a built-in modem so you can hook it right into the phone line.

Consider a program like TeleMagic as containing a simple stack of index cards each of which contains information about a store level manager, area supervisor, district manager or whomever you need to work with on your neighborhood marketing program. (See Figure 9-8.)

You may use as many index cards as you want—up to one million and quite unlike any ordinary stack of index cards, you may retrieve any card instantly, and sort and list them easily in a variety of ways.

Here's a summary of some of the marketing functions of this program:

- *Communications*
  Automatic dialer, allows for correct use of headsets, paced or automatic dialing, hold, call duration timing and

The Contact Record

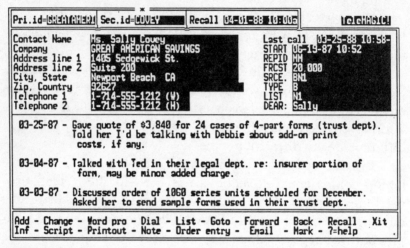

```
Pri.id=GREATAMERI Sec.id=COVEY     Recall 04-01-88 10:00a        TeleMAGIC!

Contact Name    Ms. Sally Covey              Last call  03-25-88 10:58-
Company         GREAT AMERICAN SAVINGS       START  06-19-87 10:52
Address line 1  1405 Sedgewick St.           REPID  MM
Address line 2  Suite 200                    FRCST  20,000
City, State     Newport Beach  CA            SRCE.  BN1
Zip, Country    92627                        TYPE   B
Telephone 1     1-714-555-1212 (W)           LIST   N1
Telephone 2     1-714-555-1212 (H)           DEAR:  Sally

03-25-87 - Gave quote of $3,840 for 24 cases of 4-part forms (trust dept).
           Told her I'd be talking with Debbie about add-on print
           costs, if any.

03-04-87 - Talked with Ted in their legal dept. re: insurer portion of
           form, may be minor added charge.

03-03-87 - Discussed order of 1060 series units scheduled for December.
           Asked her to send sample forms used in their trust dept.

Add - Change - Word pro - Dial - List - Goto - Forward - Back - Recall - Xit
Inf - Script - Printout - Note - Order entry - Email - Mark - ?=help
```

Figure 9-8 Diagram of a typical screen with TeleMagic. Reprinted with permission.

recording, alternate long distance services, three-way conference calling, hook, flash, etc.

- *Database*
  Fully preprogrammed to make it easy to enter, retrieve, change, display, sort, filter, virtually any kind of data.

- *Reporting*
  Use any of the many preset displays, lists, reports, plus the special "Quickie" list feature for special needs. This keeps your boss happy because you can show him or her exactly what you've been doing.

- *Calendar*
  Easily maintains lists of events, people to call back, by date and time and type of call. Keeps track of appointments, meetings, check points, ect. So when you set a time to talk to a certain manager, you merely enter the date into the "next call" line. On that day, the manager's

file pops up on the screen automatically. Push one key and you're off and running.

- *Notepad*
  Records notes about the call you made and automatically dates it. The most current notes are first. This is why you want to use a headset. With your hands free, your notes are taken right on screen and you always know what's going on with that manager.

- *Word Processing*
  Has a built-in word processor which allows instant written follow-ups after your call. The letters, memos, and notes, are dated, addressed, and personalized. This program also interfaces with other word processors.

- *Mailing*
  Creates letters or memos, labels, envelopes, and so on. Sorts in zip code sequence for bulk permit mailings too. So when you do your group memos to your managers, you can personalize it even more. Also by creating a master mailing list of participating managers you can provide them with preprinted labels so as they do promotions they send samples to everyone in the program. This makes great reinforcement to all of the managers and keeps them informed as to what others are doing.

- *Scripting*
  Since this was designed originally for telemarketing, it allows for scripting of a presentation. Though we don't use scripts as such, we do use key phrases and questions in this function to help us better work with that manager. After all you are selling them on the idea of doing these promotions.

INFORMAL GROUP TRAINING SESSION

Once a month, in each developmental market, plan on half a day when you bring all of the participating managers together with the supervisor. If it's possible to combine a few markets without creating too much expense or hassle, that's even better. Work from an agenda. Start with a review. Go around the table and have each manager and supervisor talk about what they did during the four previous months. Let them do all of the talking. You just keep the meeting running smoothly. If you get a manager who is a little shy or forgets to tell the group about a great promotion, you ask him or her about it. This prompts them to offer more information to the group.

As they review, they need to bring with them the extra samples of the printed cross-promotion pieces, fliers, newspaper coverage, and similar things. Everyone in the meeting gets copies and samples for themselves.

Next, discuss any particular difficulties any of them may have had. Open it up to the group to offer solutions. Don't act as though you know all of the answers (even though you probably do). Let them come up with their own solutions and answers with your guidance. You'll have a much better chance of success by doing so.

Sometimes they'll want to sit and complain. Let them get it out of their systems. Then, when they start repeating themselves, it's time to step in and ask the group to think of some possible means to improve the situation.

After you've done your best to deal with the difficulties, set the pace for the next month. Set the goals. Make sure you get a good variety of promotions so you may assign certain managers certain types of promotions. The three easiest ones seem to be the merchant certificates, community service donation dollars, and the value cards. Make sure a few of the stores are doing some internal contests or promotions. Some should be getting publicity. One may have a new competitor moving in, so then you start your "competitive intrusion" program.

It's important that you have a good variety of promotions to add to your arsenal so when you deliver this program in the roll-out phase to the rest of the managers in your organization, you can provide them with all of the necessary tools. Not all managers use every type of promotion. A manager's individual skills and the circumstances at the store often dictate which promotions are most appropriate for the situation. Yet, they will have had exposure to every imaginable local store promotion so they can pick and choose what will work best for them.

In addition to the variety of promotions, the other area you need to monitor carefully is the volume of promotions. The goal is for *each* manager to do at least one promotion a week. This doesn't sound like much, but you must keep the pressure on them to produce. In the first month or two, when they're most excited, you can have them do two to three a week. This would be a nice beginning.

In the first 90 days, many of the promotions won't pull as much as you want in redemption or foot traffic. Some will, however, and you must focus on the successes. The first 90 days is when your managers are trying different types of promotions, offers, partners, methods of distribution, and so on. There are numerous variables that must be looked at. Once you know what works, your success ratio rapidly goes higher.

This is the reason why the monthly group sessions are important. Once you have a success with one manager, share that story with the others. See how well that success translates into success for all the others. Also, see how some of the other managers take that success and make it even better or adapt it to a unique situation. This is how your program builds.

At the end of the first year, your program is filled with nothing but success. Before you even begin your roll-out, you have a program that gets results.

ROLLING IT OUT

With your program fully developed and your prototype market(s) in place, you're now ready to roll out the program to your organization. Each organization has its own way of getting a new program out to the store level, and this one would be much like introducing a new product. There are, however, some key elements that are important.

First, if possible, conduct your new seminar for the supervisors first. Then let them have a little time to implement a few of the programs on their own. You might follow up on the supervisor level, just as you did with your participating managers. Once you have your supervisors successfully understanding and implementing some of this program, the chances of the managers doing it properly are much higher.

Secondly, you might consider rolling it out on a market-by-market basis. This way you can control the quality of the growth of the program better, yet the roll-out phase can take a great deal longer. You did take one year to develop your program, and it's very possible that upper management will want to start reaping the rewards a little sooner.

The roll out is not really the difficult part. I suggest that it be done with a series of seminars. Perhaps you can launch it at your annual convention, with an in-depth seminar to follow in the field. A videotape is another possibility; they're good for reinforcement or bringing on a new manager once the program is in place. To get your entire organization into this program, live seminars work the best.

The difficult part is the follow up. You'll be relying on your supervisors to do in the field what you did for the development phase. This means that you'll be working with the supervisors on the same level as you did your developmental managers. In even larger organizations, you may find that you're dealing with the second level supervisors.

Another important element for success is that all your managers, area supervisors, and district managers have to have some type of performance-based bonus program for them to be motivated to go to all of this extra effort. Most managers are on a bonus program that considers increased sales as well as certain criteria on expenses and quality. You need a fair bonus program because there has to be an incentive for these managers to work at the program.

Also, once you roll out the program, it takes constant maintenance to make sure it continues to work for you. As Michael LeBoeuf points out in his book *The Greatest Management Principle*, "what gets rewarded gets done." In addition to the regular compensation, you also need to recognize outstanding streetsmart marketing efforts. At your annual convention, have awards for various types of local promotions. Recognize managers in the newsletter or whatever vehicles you have.

Once you have it rolled out, constantly update the program. The program you have three years from now will be much more improved than the one you have when you first roll it out. It's a never-ending battle to improve it and make it better.

When you're at that point, no one can touch you. Your managers own the turf around their store. They're working with area merchants, major employers, organizations, charity groups, the news media, the local advertising media, their own employees, and even their own customers. Every possible local avenue is used to network in that community and supplement all of the national and regional marketing and advertising you give them. After all, no matter how much you advertise, it all boils down to how the customer is treated when they visit your store for the first time.

POST ROLL-OUT

Once you have your program totally implemented throughout your system, you need to incorporate your program into your normal management training because most organizations have a certain amount of store manager attribution and growth.

If you won't be conducting this seminar live, your next best bet is to videotape one of your full-day seminars. Then you can use the video along with your workbook for getting new managers up to speed. A video isn't nearly as effective as a live seminar, and for that reason, I prefer doing the national roll-out with a series of live seminars. But once you have your program working in the field, it's much easier to bring a new manager on. A video, workbook, and trained facilitator works fine.

As mentioned before, you'll want to continually upgrade your program as well as add some new sections. Over a period of a few years, you'll perhaps want special modules for special situations such as grand openings, competitive intrusion, manager replacement, and so on. As you see a growing need for a specialized adaptation for your store, you can create a one to three-hour seminar that addresses those particular issues.

With these specialized seminars, you don't need to address the basics of your streetsmart marketing program, but rather how to apply what they've learned in their basic program, along with specialized ideas in an effort to deal with the problem at hand. You may find that a one-hour mini seminar and brief handout is all that is needed.

Other areas of specialization that you may want to address in the years following your national rollout are urban store vs. rural store, inner city vs. interstate, minority communities, and so on.

When you have a new product or service introduction as part of the marketing and advertising portion of the introduction, include a special streetsmart checklist of techniques that managers can do on the store level to help with the new program. Getting support on the store level can really make or break the introduction for a new product or service, so have the "machinery" in place first and you'll see that you can plug in many things.

Epilogue

This book is just the first step to getting your own streetsmart marketing program developed and implemented in your organization. Now comes the hard work and only you can do it.

It took over 10 years to gather and fine tune these ideas and techniques. They work. Each one of them has been done a number of times by a variety of types of business. But now, it's up to you. This is where most local store marketing programs fail. It's not for lack of ideas . . . but rather lack of execution and commitment.

Think about it? What else could your organization do to make this large an impact for so little money? Absolutely nothing. If you have 500 stores, then this program, in addition to all of your regular advertising and marketing efforts, gives you 500 salespeople . . . 500 representatives of your company in 500 different neighborhoods and communities where you do your business. It is geographically and demographically focused so there is a minimal of wasted effort.

Sure, they'll be some things that don't work, but that's how you eventually come up with your own plan of attack that does. Many people in your organization may try to shoot down the program. They do this because it's perhaps not glamorous like producing slick TV spots or full color magazine ads. You're asking your local managers to do more work, to take initiative—that always raises eyebrows. Deal with it.

Don't look at this program as the end all. It's not. It can make you more competitive for less dollars but you still have to satisfy the needs of your customers. If you do that, your street-fighting efforts will pay off handsomely . . . in time.

As you go out there and do these programs, you'll no doubt run into others doing the same. Some are doing it right, others are not. After all, we've been preaching this program for the past 10 years. But each neighborhood is different. Each area is up for grabs.

A regional or local fast-food operation may not be able to compete with McDonald's on a national basis and they certainly have a lot of advantages going for them but when you get right down to it, they have to pull customers from the same neighborhood as you do. Get down in the trenches and fight for your share of the pie . . . or the cake . . . or the ice cream, whichever has the biggest margins that week.

Resource Guide

Note: For your convenience, the phone numbers of the resources are listed when available. These numbers are current as of this writing but because phone numbers often change, you may have to go through directory assistance for any numbers that have changed.

BOOKS

The Great Brain Robbery by Murray Raphel and Ray Considine
    Self-published
    Murray Raphel Advertising. Gordon's Alley, Atlantic City, NJ 08401
    609/348-6646
    Interesting stories and techniques for getting new customers. Fun to read and opens with some great examples of what we would call some super "streetfighters."

Positioning: The Battle for the Mind by Jack Trout and Al Riese
    To be successful you need to know and take advantage of your unique nitche in the marketplace. This book is a "must read."

The Greatest Management Principle in the World by Dr. Michael LeBoeuf
(New York: Berkley Publishing Group)

Teaches you how to get other people to do what you want them to do based on the principle: The things that get rewarded get done.

How to Win Customers and Keep them for Life by Dr. Michael LeBoeuf
(New York: Berkley Publishing Group)

The ultimate customers service book. Take the concepts from *Greatest Management Principle* and applies them to keeping your customers happy.

Working Smart by Dr. Michael LeBoeuf
(New York: Warner Books)

Time management and goal setting techniques. Also available in audio.

The Unabashed Self-Promoters Guide by Jeffrey L. Lant
Self-published
50 Follen Street, Suite 507, Cambridge, MA 02138
617/547-6372

Ideas and techniques for promoting yourself. Helpful when you adapt it to selling yourself to your field management as a consultant and adviser.

Guerrilla Marketing by Jay Conrad Levinson
(Boston, MA: Houghton Mifflin)

Deals with low-cost marketing, mass media advertising and research techniques.

Phone Power by George Walther
Available from the author: 401 Second Avenue South, Suite 70, Seattle, WA 98104
800/843-8353

Shows you how to get the most out of your phone.

Power Speaks by Dorothy Leeds
Available from the author: Organizational Technologies, Inc., 800 West End Avenue, Suite 10A, NY 10025
212/864-2424

Smart Questions by Dorothy Leeds
Available from the author: Organizational Technologies, Inc., 800 West End Avenue, Suite 10A, NY 10025
212/864-2424

Successful Telephone Selling in the 80's by Martin D. Shafiroff and Robert L. Shook
Techniques for selling by telephone.

Perfect Sales Presentation by Robert L. Shook
(New York: Bantam Books)
Helps you learn sales from some of the nation's top salespeople.

How To Close Any Sale by Joe Girard and Robert L. Shook
(New York: Warner Books)
Sales techniques.

Streetfighting: Low Cost Advertising/Promotions for Your Business by Jeff Slutsky
Available from the author: Retail Marketing Institute, 34 West Whittier Street, Columbus, OH 43206
614/443-5555
The predecessor to *StreetSmart Marketing*, you'll find more anecdotes and examples of successful promotions plus four chapters geared to getting the most from your radio, TV, outdoor, and print advertising.

Streetfighter's Neighborhood Sales Builders Workbook by Jeff Slutsky
Self-published
Available from the author: Retail Marketing Institute, 34 West Whittier Street, Columbus, OH 43206
614/443-5555

100-page workbook that takes you step-by-step through creating your own local marketing plan geared specifically for your type of business and the neighborhood you serve.

The 33 Secrets of StreetSmart Tele-Selling by Jeff Slutsky and Marc Slutsky
Available after June, 1989 from the authors: Retail Marketing Institute, 34 West Whittier Street, Columbus, OH 43206
614/443-5555
Teaches you a Streetfighter's approach to telemarketing.

AUDIO CASSETTE ALBUMS

We recommend the use of audio cassette albums whenever possible. From a time-management standpoint, it's the only medium for learning that can be used in almost any situation including driving in your car, flying, and exercising.

The Greatest Management Principle in the World by Dr. Michael LeBoeuf
Teaches you how to get other people to do what you want them to do based on the principle: The things that get rewarded get done.

How to Win Customers and Keep them for Life by Dr. Michael LeBoeuf
6 cassette tapes
Nightingale-Conant Corporation, 7300 North Lehigh Avenue, Chicago, IL 60648
800/323-5552
Customer service is critical for any business to be successful. Without it, your marketing efforts can only run you out of business faster!

Working Smarter by Dr. Michael LeBoeuf
6 cassette tapes

Nightingale-Conant Corporation (see previous listing)
800/323-5552

A good time management/goal setting program for getting the most out of your time.

Phone Power by George Walther
Nightingale-Conant Corporation (see previous listing)
13 individual cassettes which can be ordered separately or as a "Power Pack" which gets you the videotape, free. Available from the author: 401 Second Avenue South, Suite 70, Seattle, WA 98104
800/843-8353

The individual tapes cover different concepts including: Phone Power for the Person Who Manages, for Effective Communications, for the Receptionist, for the Switchboard Operator, for the Secretary, for the Outbound Telemarketer, for the Inbound Telemarketer, for Negotiation, for Dealing with Difficult People, for the Customer Service Professional, for the Salesperson, for Getting Appointments, for the Accounts Receivable Collector.

Profitable Telemarketing: Total Training for Professional Excellence by George Walther
6 cassette tapes
Available from the author: 401 Second Avenue South, Suite 70, Seattle, WA 98104
800/843-8353

Teaches you how to use the telephone to increase sales.

Power Speak by Dorothy Leeds
6 cassette tapes
Available from the author: Organizational Technologies, Inc., 800 West End Avenue, Suite 10A, New York, NY 10025
212/864-2424

Communication is always critical to helping you get your ideas across. Speaking to a larger group is important to your group training efforts. This book teaches you how to do that effectively.

Smart Questions by Dorothy Leeds
Available after June, 1989 from the author: Organizational Technologies, Inc., 800 West End Avenue, Suite 10A, NY 10025
212/864-2424

Ways you can get what you want by learning what others really want from you.

Prime Prospects Unlimited (formally *Gold Calling*) by Bill Bishop
Self-published
8 audio cassettes

This program is primarily for helping outside salespeople convert their door-to-door cold calling to setting up good qualified appointments. Many of the ideas in this program were used for our tele-consulting techniques in Chapter 9.
Available from the author: 834 Gran Paseo Drive, Orlando, FL 32825
407/281-1395.

Stalls Are for Horses, Not Sales People by Bill Bishop
Self-published
2 audio cassettes

Techniques for getting people to make a decision and get off of dead center. Helpful in working with customers or store managers when conducting field consulting.
Available from the author: (see previous listing)
407/281-1395

Million Dollar Presentations (replaces the *Million Dollar Close* program) by Bill Bishop

Some of the most effective sales and communications techniques you'll find.

Available June, 1989 from the author: (see previous listing)
407/281-1395

Managing a Retail Staff to Success by Harry Friedman
Self-published
Available from the author: 8636 Sepulveda Blvd, Suite C,
Los Angeles, CA 90045
800/351-8040

Once you get them in the front door, you have to buy or
your advertising and marketing is wasted. This program
helps you manage your sales staff.

Successful Retail Selling by Harry Friedman
Self-published
Available from the author: (see previous listing)
800/351-8040

Techniques for getting the customer to buy once they're
already in your store.

Streetfighter's Neighborhood Sales Builders by Jeff Slutsky
6 tapes/100-page workbook
Available from Retail Marketing Institute, 34 West Whittier
Street, Columbus, OH 43206
614/443-5555

Recorded live at a full-day seminar, teaches you step-by-
step the complete Streetfighting program. It comes with the
Streetfighter's Workbook which becomes your customized
plan of attack.

The 33 Secrets of StreetSmart Tele-Selling by Jeff Slutsky and
Marc Slutsky
(Englewood Cliffs, NJ: Prentice-Hall)
3 tapes/workbook, available after June 1989
614/443-5555

Provides you a streetfighter's approach to telephone selling
techniques.

VIDEOS

Video training programs are often the most effective way to comprehension of information. They require more attention than an audio program and can provide you the maximum amount of information in the shortest period of time.

How to Win Customers and Keep Them for Life by Dr. Michael LeBoeuf
(Hollywood, CA: Cally Curtis Company)
Purchase price $575, rental $130, can be ordered through the author
504/833-8873

The Greatest Management Principle in the World by Dr. Michael LeBoeuf
(Deerfield, IL: Coronet/MTI Film & Video)
800/621-2131
Three different programs available. Teaches you how to get other people to do what you want them to do based on the principle: The things that get rewarded get done.

Smart Questions by Dorothy Leeds
American Marketing Association
Available after June, 1989 from the author: Organizational Technologies, Inc., 800 West End Avenue, Suite 10A, New York, NY 10025
212/864-2424

Phone Power Video by George Walther
Available from the author: 401 Second Avenue South, Suite 70, Seattle, WA 98104
800/843-8353
$54.95 or free when you order all 13 of the *Phone Power* audio cassettes. A great overview of the entire "phone power" concept.

Prime Prospects Unlimited (formally *Gold Calling*) by Bill Bishop
Self-published, 1 VHS tape

This program is primarily for helping outside salespeople convert their door-to-door cold calling to setting up good qualified appointments. Many of the ideas in this program were used for our tele-consulting techniques in Chapter 9.
Available from the author: 834 Gran Paseo Drive, Orlando, FL 32825
407/281-1395

Stalls Are for Horses, Not Sales People by Bill Bishop
Self-published, 1 VHS tape.

Techniques for getting people to make a decision and get off of dead center. Helpful in working with customers or store managers when conducting field consulting.
Available from the author: (see previous listing)
407/281-1395

Managing a Retail Staff to Success by Harry Friedman
Self-published
Available from the author: 8636 Sepulveda Blvd, Suite C, Los Angeles, CA 90045
800/351-8040

Teaches you have to manage your salesforce so you can get better results.

Successful Retail Selling by Harry Friedman
Self-published
Available from the author: (see previous listing)
800/351-8040

Teaches your salesforce how to better sell.

Streetfighter's Profit Package by Jeff Slutsky
Package contains 1 VHS, *The Complete Neighborhood Sales Builders* audio album with workbook.

Streetfighting: Low Cost Advertising/Promotion for Your Business and *Streetfighter's Advance Training Manual.* $389
Retail Marketing Institute, 34 West Whittier Street, Columbus, OH 43206
614/443-5555

Streetfighter's Tele-Selling by Jeff Slutsky and Marc Slutsky
1 VHS/workbook, available after June 1989
Retail Marketing Institute, 34 West Whittier Street, Columbus, OH 43206
614/443-5555

Provides you a streetfighter's approach to telephone selling techniques.

OTHER RESOURCES

These resources are suggested for your convenience and to help you develop and implement your streetfighting program as effectively and efficiently as possible. In some cases, we were provided samples to use and review but other than that we receive no payments, royalties, or commission. These are suggested because we feel your program will be enhanced by their use.

TeleMagic Telemarketing Computer Software by Michael McCafferty
Computer software for single user or multi-user telemarketing program. Requires MS DOS, suggested machine requires are 640K RAM, 20 meg hard drive, modem. Can work on 2 diskette drives and 512K RAM. Published by Remote Control Computer Support Group, 514 Via de la Valle, Suite 306, Solana Beach, CA 92075
800/992-9952 or 619/481-8577

Head sets of professional quality Allows for hands-free operation. Especially good for field marketing people who need to contact numerous neighborhood level managers during

the development and implementation phase of a neighborhood marketing program. Some retail operations using
tele-selling techniques will also find this very useful. Must
use professional quality headsets. Available from Plantron-
ics, 345 Encinal Street, Santa Cruz, CA 95060
800/662-3902 (in California) 800/538-0748 (outside
California)

Archer Telephone Recorder Allows you to record your own telephone conversations. Plugs into any cassette recorder with
a remote plug. Starts recording when you pick up the hand-
set and stops when you hang up. Great for helping you
review and improving your tele-consulting or tele-selling
skills. Available at Radio Shack.

Duophone Computerized Phone Accountant Tracks all incoming
and outgoing calls on calculator tape. Tells you length of
each call, time, date, and can code calls. If you're doing a lot
of calling, this can be very helpful. Not necessary if you use
TeleMagic. Good only on one line at a time (unless you get
more units). Available at Radio Shack.

The Lynx System This modular wall planner of "T" cards is the
perfect status board. At a glance you can see the status of
store managers and their Streetfighting marketing efforts.
You can customize it to suit your specific needs by size of
the cards and number of rows of cards. Price can vary from
$40 to $500 depending on what you need. Get their catalog
to see how this might help you. Available through Remark-
able Products. 245 Pegasus Avenue. Northvale, NJ 07647
201/784-0900

Annual Planning Wall Calender Our favorite is the Smart Chart
by John Lee Companies. PO Box 398R, Crawfordsville, FL
32327
904/926-7122
They also provide some very helpful hints on using this
calender most effectively.

Index